The Good Indian'

V. RAGHUNATHAN is an academic, corporate executive, author, columnist and a hobbyist. He has made Bengaluru his home.

He taught finance at the Indian Institute of Management, Ahmedabad, for a couple of decades before turning a banker as the president of ING Vysya Bank in Bengaluru; the director of the Schulich School of Business (India Campus, York University, Toronto, Canada); and the CEO of GMR Varalakshmi Foundation. He continues to pursue his academic interests as an adjunct professor at the University of Bocconi in Milan, Italy, and the Schulich School of Business, York University, in Toronto, Canada.

He has been writing extensively for leading newspapers and magazines and currently blogs for the *Times of India*.

Raghu has probably the largest collection of antique locks in the country, has played chess at the all-India level, and was briefly a cartoonist for a national daily.

The Good Indian's Guide to Queue-jumping

V. Raghunathan

HarperCollins *Publishers* India

First published in India in 2016 by
HarperCollins *Publishers* India

Copyright © V. Raghunathan 2016

P-ISBN: 978-93-5029-674-5
E-ISBN: 978-93-5029-681-3

2 4 6 8 10 9 7 5 3 1

V. Raghunathan asserts the moral right to be identified
as the author of this work.

HarperCollins *Publishers*
A-75, Sector 57, Noida, Uttar Pradesh 201301, India
1 London Bridge Street, London, SE1 9GF, United Kingdom
Hazelton Lanes, 55 Avenue Road, Suite 2900, Toronto, Ontario M5R 3L2
and 1995 Markham Road, Scarborough, Ontario M1B 5M8, Canada
25 Ryde Road, Pymble, Sydney, NSW 2073, Australia
195 Broadway, New York, NY 10007, USA

Typeset in 11/15 Palatino Linotype at
SÜRYA, New Delhi

Printed and bound at
Thomson Press (India) Ltd.

To
The queue of my siblings (two ahead and two behind)
Uma, Rama, Shyama and Ravi

Contents

1

The Wisdom of Queues

It was the day of the big sale. Rumours of the great deals (and some advertising in the local papers) were the main reason for the long line that formed in front of the store well before 8:30 a.m., the store's opening time.

A small man pushed his way to the front of the line, only to be pushed back amid loud and colourful curses. On the man's second attempt, he was punched square in the jaw, knocked around a bit and then thrown to the end of the line again.

As he got up the second time, he said to the person at the end of the line, 'That does it! If they hit me one more time, I'm not opening the store!'

It is well known that the universe is not a place that is either constant or predictable. Quantum mechanics tells us it is not. It is not even orderly, if you go by the laws of thermodynamics, which tell us that 'the universe is tending towards maximum entropy', or headed towards maximal 'disorder'. Well, if so, don't our fluid, fuzzy and often chaotic queues contribute more to the natural order of the universe? So why does the world often baulk at our frequent jumping of queues when it is patently clear that ours is a civilization closer to nirvana, for we, including our inherent reservations against queuing, flow with the forces of the universe?

A wise man is supposed to have said, 'Half of life is showing up. The other half is waiting in line.' Can't disagree with that – certainly not we who spend half our lives waiting in queues and the other half scheming how to jump them.

Those of us who lost our milk teeth in the 1960s and '70s may recall two-year-long queues for HMT watches and decade-long ones for a classic black rotary-dial phone, a Bajaj scooter or a Fiat car. And for basic justice from the courts, we have waited even longer and continue to do so.

My familiarity with queues has only increased with time. I recall a time in the 1980s when, come summer, I would be dispatched to the railway station for advance reservation of the family's journey from Punjab to Tamil Nadu. I would be armed with a dhurrie – a heavy cotton rug – an inflatable pillow and a mottled glass bottle (of Kissan Squash) of water, charged to sleep in the line in front of the railway reservation counters waiting for the gates to open, virtually making an event of it, with packed dinner and breakfast to boot. I recall this being the ritual for a US visa as well. Even the queues for gas cylinders and at shops were impressively long. And of course, much of my life has been spent witnessing or experiencing queues at railway stations; queues at municipal water taps; queues at bus stops; queues at taxi stands; queues outside cinema halls; queues at ration shops; queues at airports – whether departure gates, airline counters, security gates or boarding gates; queues outside RTO offices; queues outside passport offices; queues at hospitals; queues outside restaurants; queues for voting; queues for admitting toddlers into nursery schools; queues at McDonald's; queues at toll gates on our newfangled highways – in short, queues pretty much anywhere. The truth is, most of us, with the exception of most VVIPs and at one time the likes of Robert Vadra, are rarely far from a queue.

It may be that before the 1990s queues were largely driven by shortage on the supply side of goods and services while today they are mostly driven by excess of demand. But queues are, and almost always have been, a part of our lives – as participants, as onlookers, and as sufferers.

Search for the Origin of Queues

When did queues first come into being as a social protocol? Did they exist in the primitive world? Where was the earliest known queue formed? Did they exist in ancient India? When did a queuing culture first take root in human society?

The last is a searching question – even if, strictly speaking, an anthropological and not a sociological one. Be that as it may, I have spent some time hunting and gathering information on the Internet looking for the origins of queuing in the history of humanity. I was about to give up when I saw a news item emanating from our own continent, in an issue of the *China Daily*: 'Archaeological evidence suggests Chinese people once queued.'[1] And the somewhat controversial report wasn't referring to the 'queues' at the back of the heads of Chinese gentlemen.*

According to the report, archaeologists excavating near Yinxu – the capital of the Shang Dynasty (1766-1050 BC) in the east of the country, about 500 kilometres from Beijing – had made a most remarkable discovery: fossilized remains of three people, one behind the other, as if they were in a queue. Well, that's the oldest evidence I have been able to trace of Homo sapiens standing in queues, if this is evidence indeed. According to this report, Dr Charles Whitmore, a visiting palaeontologist with the Chinese Academy of Sciences, believed that the discovery had led to 'a paradigm shift in our understanding of the Chinese people.' According to him, 'The scientific community has long believed Chinese people to be genetically unwilling to file singly' (so we in India can take heart). But, following this discovery, he believed that this opinion about the Chinese unwillingness to queue up may have been wrong, given that once upon a time they did stand in line quite patiently. Dr Whitmore particularly rued the fact that even though thirty centuries ago the Chinese may have possessed the good sense to align one behind the other, today such linear formations are observed only in 'insufferably precise military exercises and firing squads'!

------

*The long braided pigtails which Chinese men wore in the days of yore were also referred to as 'queues'.

But in China there are serious challengers to Whitmore's finding. Since China is a communist country and a regulated society, the social attitudes there to queues differ from those in the West, where regulation stems from other roots. That's why sceptics like Professor Shi-mian Maifu of Beijing Normal University refuse to 'rush into conclusions here'. Shi-mian believes there could be other explanations for the linear alignment of the three ancestors: like a dance (retro-Bollywood?), or a practical joke, and urges Westerners to 'stand still' and 'remain calm' before rushing to declare their finding as if it were an anthropological milestone like the Java Man[2]. Says Professor Shi-mian with some emphasis, 'I cannot believe that any reasonable, sane Chinese person would choose to purposefully increase the time he or she spends waiting out of deference to someone else.' He refuses to stand behind that line of logic.

But either way both parties seem convinced that today the Chinese stand united in their dislike for forming queues, which provides us some consolation in our own country. So all those who believe that China and India cannot be spoken about in the same breath when it comes to wealth creation, infrastructure, manufacturing, exports, imports, infant mortality, or virtually any parameter of a country's development, will have to reconcile themselves to the fact that the two countries do share a common antipathy to queues. One expatriate fumes in a blog thus: 'The Chinese solution [to queues] is to pretend that you are the only person in the room, and that you are the most important person in the world. You angle your elbows out and simply shove anyone in the way aside.' Well, some may say ditto about us too.

However, our main concern here is the innate sociological attitude to queues in China. The reality in more recent times in that country is that you queue when you are *asked*, or even *expected*, to queue. For example, it is not uncommon to observe even airline crew walking to the aircraft in a rigid line, and not in groups as we often see elsewhere. One understands this is to discourage too much idle chatter among employees, which is the cauldron in which most social revolutions brew in their early days. The state *expects* the crew to walk up to the aircraft in a line, and so they do.

Queues in India

The ancient origins, if any, of queuing in India are lost in the mists of time. None of our sociological, anthropological or historical records guide us in this respect. It may be that as early as the Mohenjo-daro and Harappa civilizations we used to queue, just as we used to have closed drains, but lost the ability to queue later just as we lost the propensity to make closed sewers.

But as we have already seen, more recent evidence of queues in India is aplenty. Most of us in this subcontinent are experts in lining up, even if our attitude towards queues is a little fluid, laissez-faire or even a bit permissive. It is as if we participate in a queue against the cry of our nature. Some weak voice in our hearts tells us to queue, but then our primal nature yells at us to turn around 180 degrees, and our attitude in the queue seems to be the result of the two forces, as it were.

On occasion we would appear almost disciplined in the queues; but then, on other occasions, our queues are an unholy cross between the Kumbh Mela and Dalal Street of the 1980s. We may be patient enough to suffer ten- and twenty-year queues for the most ordinary requirements of life without thinking of turning revolutionaries, unlike Russians, for example (it was the impoverished women of St Petersburg queuing up for bread on a cold, snowbound February day in 1917 who led to the abdication of the czar, triggering off the Russian Revolution), but will impatiently rush to jump a red light, endangering our own lives and those of others.

Russians may have been impatient with queuing for bread and may have responded with a revolution. But in our ancient land, we are not given to revolt for flippant, or even for non-flippant, reasons. After all, didn't our forefathers allow the Mongols, the Mughals, the Dutch, the French, the British and half a dozen other invaders of the world to rule us for nearly eight centuries without a single revolt, until 1857 may be? True, we did come close to another revolution very recently, thanks to Anna Hazare. But the truth is, our infinite patience with corruption snuffed out the sparks set off by Anna before they built up into a raging flame.

What is more, this trait is perhaps the most secular and non-parochial of all our traits. Hindus, Muslims, Christians, Sikhs, Buddhists, Jains and may be even our Jews; Punjabis, Assamese, Bengalis, Tamils, Maharashtrians or those from a score of other states – irrespective of caste or creed – all of them jump lines with the same traditional gaiety and fervour with which we are supposed to celebrate Holi nationwide, showing the same disdain for queues that dogs reserve for lamp posts. Preventing either from doing what they are wont to would be a disruption of Mother Nature.

Why Do We Jump Queues?

Any discussion on queue-jumping immediately prompts the question: 'Why do Indians jump queues?' Well, the truth is we are not the only people in the world who jump queues. But yes, the spirit of that question is clear: we know deep down that we probably jump queues more than most other peoples in the world, and so would like to know why.

The only answer to the general question 'Why do people jump queues?' is clearly that they desire to be attended faster than those who came before them for the same service. And if we think we jump queues more than most, why, our desire to be served ahead of our compatriots before us in the line must be a tad stronger than that of most other people in the world. But why is it so? Are we a nation of far more competitive citizens than the rest of the world? But if so, why are we laggards when it comes to most parameters of achievement?

But, of course, this kind of answer that throws back a set of counter-questions leaves us dissatisfied. The dissatisfaction, I suspect, is not with the answer's failure to help us improve our behaviour. Deep down, I suspect that we don't even want to 'improve' our behaviour. What we would like is to see some 'socio-economic' justification – like shortages, population, poverty, illiteracy, or maybe colonialism, and so on (even if we are personally well-educated, well-off, suffer no privations and born in free

India) – so that none of us needs to feel directly responsible or ashamed of this trait.

We want some clean, rational and easy-to-accept set of justifications that would amply explain why we jump queues more than most without suffering any sense of shame, guilt and culpability. Basically, the answer should be such that it does not prevent us from jumping queues and at the same time gives us a good reason to justify our behaviour, so that we can walk tall, head held high, in the comity of nations.

Sadly, in this framework, the question above is difficult to answer, at least not in a way that can lead us to curb our tendency to queue-jump. Could we be shamed out of queue-jumping? This is difficult to achieve without being labelled an 'India basher' – a favourite term we reserve for anyone trying to hold a mirror to our collective behaviour (please see the box at the end of this chapter).

Queue-jumping and Shortages

If you are among those who believe queue-jumping is the direct consequence of shortages, you probably belong to a healthy majority, as any number of intellectuals and non-intellectuals alike do seem to hold that view.

The refrain usually runs thus: We are a country of 1.3 billion, and much as we would like to believe otherwise, we are still predominantly a country of shortages – shortage of food, shortage of health services, shortage of quality primary, secondary and tertiary educational institutions, shortage of skilled manpower, shortage of service windows and much else besides. So having been conditioned to shortages for centuries, it is no wonder that we jump queues even when the conditions may have changed (which, of course, begs the well-worn question: if the tendency is so ingrained in us, how is it that we behave properly as soon as we travel outside the country? We shall answer that question a little later in the book).

But as the author of a compendium on queue-jumping, I beg to differ. Take the former Soviet Union for example. Shortages were endemic, and hence queues historically long, in the countries once part of the Union. But they are far from being nations of queue-jumpers. Of course, we may chalk up their discipline to their despotic regime, while chalking up our chaotic queue etiquette to democracy's account, overlooking the implied admission that we would *behave* only if someone held a gun to our gullet, or at least a baton to our butt.

I beg to disagree with the notion that queue-jumping is a consequence of shortages. It is the queue, and more particularly its length, that could be said to be the direct consequence of shortages. In other words, as India has been a shortage economy for decades, long queues may certainly have become an integral part of our lives.

But *queue-jumping*, when the queue is comprised of co-sufferers of shortages, can hardly be justified by reasons of shortages alone, especially in situations where the shortage is not a life-and-death issue. What is involved here is the lack of an elementary sense of fairness amongst a people in realizing that those who came before them ought to be served ahead of them.

No wonder the disregard for queues also found its way into the very folklore of the nation via Bollywood when Amitabh Bachchan growled in his bass voice in *Kaalia* (1981), '*Hum jahan khade ho jaate hain, line wahin se shuru hoti hai,*', saying in effect – I will always jump to the head of the queue; stop me if you dare.

We believe that shortages and the resulting queues justify our propensity for queue-jumping. What is more, it is as if other factors also don't matter – educated or not; wealthy or not; whether or not services are guaranteed. What else could explain educated people belonging to the higher socio-economic strata jumping queues at airports when they have an assured seat at the time of boarding? Could it be the shortage of bin space for bags, given our penchant for not travelling light? But then what explains their mad rush while disembarking? What purpose does it serve to get up from one's seat and rush ahead even before the aircraft has come to a halt? Why are we not mindful of the fact that it is only decorous, let alone fair, that those seated in front of us are allowed to disembark first?

Even when there is no shortage per se of a service being offered, we often create artificial shortages, and hence long queues, by keeping the service windows few and far between. It is as if we lack the basic respect for our fellow citizens.

For example, even when there are enough berths in our trains to go around on a particular route, the railway authorities often operate very few ticketing windows – even a single window at times – causing artificially long lines.

Adding one or two extra windows or X-ray machines for baggage screening could cut the queues significantly. The same is true of airline counters as well as any number of other queues. And once the queues become long, they are fertile ground for rampant queue-jumping.

Does our propensity for fewer service windows stem from thinking that more windows means more manpower? Or could it be that our mindset allows us to afford comfort only to the privileged few – why waste precious resources on simple comforts like shorter lines for the common folk? Why exert to add another window when we can get by without doing anything at all, even if we are empowered to add that window? After all, we would be paid the same at the end of the month and there will be no medal to pin on the lapel for the effort in either case. There is little respect for the ordinary man on the street.

The same disrespect for our fellow beings manifests at higher levels as well, in not empowering officials lower down who could make a difference. How can we trust a functionary below us in rank with such powers? After all, as everybody knows, power is only for the top few, right? Add it all up several times over and it results in a disempowered system all the way up and down, with a few slow and poor service windows disrespectful of their own people.

I recall the days when the US consulates in many Indian cities kept only a single window functional under conditions of sun, rain and wind for returning passports after the approval of visas even if it meant people had to wait around in long queues for several hours. This may be disrespectful of us as a people, and rather tiresome, but why do we do the same to ourselves, unless we have a masochistic streak running amongst us?

We can view ourselves as part of the whole, that is, as members of a larger society. Or we can view ourselves – as I, me, myself – as standalone entities. If we take the first view, we have no option but to learn to follow queues as a civilized society, if only to bring a modicum of order to our social behaviour in an over-populated country. On the other hand, if we take the second view, we simply must get better at jumping queues for sheer survival. Of course, when every single Indian has read this book, we will all be back to where we are, with no one with an edge. How likely that scenario could be I leave it to you to postulate.

But whether we are part of a whole or standalone entities, I believe that we in India have evolved some wisdom of our own about queue-jumping, and the objective of this book is to enhance that wisdom.

The Wisdom of 'Counter-Queue-jumping'

I have come across the following example of wisdom in those well-meaning, sugary email forwards that we all receive in abundance. It in fact turns queue-jumping on its head. It involves voluntarily going to the end of the queue – or, counter-queue-jumping. The stated instance is ascribed to various nationalities, ranging from Swedish to Japanese, depending on the society that the sender wishes to eulogize. While the details vary, the example largely unfolds as follows:

I was in Sweden/Japan/any other place for the first time on work/leisure. Winter was just setting in and it was cold. One of my friends would pick me up from the hotel and take me out to various places of interest. Often as we arrived early at her company office/theatre/opera, I noticed that she would park the car far away from the entrance and we would have to walk a longer distance than if we had parked closer. At first, I didn't react. Not even the second or the third time.

But at last, not able to contain my curiosity, I asked her, 'Do you have a fixed parking space even at a theatre?'

'Of course not.'

'Then why do you park so far from the entrance even when there is plenty of free parking available in the parking lot?'

'Since we're here early, we have all the time to walk, don't we? Don't you think that those who are late need to park closer to the entry point?'

I have not personally encountered this wisdom in my travels. But even if the cited example is a pure figment of a good Samaritan's imagination, it is a good example nevertheless of the wisdom of 'counter queue-jumping', just as we have our wisdom of jumping queues.

Another question we can ask is whether the root cause of our queue-jumping is our enormous population. But if long queues were to be the reason for queue-jumping, one should see a great deal of it outside the Louvre or Versailles or the Vatican or the Buckingham Palace, all of whom always have queues longer than any of ours.

While we shall look into factors like education, level of wealth and a whole range of other variables that could possibly influence a people's queue-jumping behaviour, prima facie it would seem that as far as we are concerned, it is a well-waggled potpourri of a bit of shortages blended with an overdose of population, a pinch of our innate nature, a dash of our nurture and a good sprinkling of our general aversion to abide by systems, which I explain at some length in my book *Games Indians Play*.[3] And perhaps the aforementioned admixture is also seasoned with our generous indifference to the idea of fairness towards fellow beings, which perhaps arises as much from over-population as from our deep-rooted selfishness – also dealt with at some length in the same book.

True, a lack of education and preponderance of poverty may be seen to be major forces behind the trait of queue-jumping. But it is to offset the effects of shortages, education or economic well-being that in the chapters ahead I shall keep falling back on the examples of queuing behaviour at airports, where seats are assured and specified, leaving no scope for shortages, and travellers are educationally and economically well above the national average, so that we do not single out the uneducated and the poor for queue-jumping behaviour.

In my worldview, queue-jumping is not so much a function of shortages, education or poverty as the result of the combined weight of our attitudes to fairness, care and concern for others, etiquette, discipline, opportunity cost, values and self-regulation (or the lack of it), not to mention the prevalence or otherwise of regulation, its implementation, penalties, fines, fees, systems and processes to manage queues.

What's the Problem with Jumping Queues?

As a staunch nationalist and a patriotic Indian endowed with the gift of the gab, I am ready to take offence at any hint that queue-jumping is one of our national traits which reflects poorly on our civility as a society. Are intelligent human beings really wired to stand in queues and enjoy the experience, especially when they are at the tail end of a long queue at the counter of the regional transport office for the renewal of their driving licence? If not, how can lines be so central to a civilized society? Just because queues are innately ordered, intrinsically fair to all and egalitarian?

In any case, who decides that lines are necessary for a civilized society? After all, don't we belong to an ancient civilization and don't we jump queues? Isn't that proof enough that civilized people do jump queues? Who can vouchsafe what came first: the queue or the civilization? It may be that in Western countries lines came up first and shaped their civilization. In India, my ancient civilization has chosen to be foggy about queues. So who is to question the sophistication of my civilization just because I choose to jump queues where and when I fancy?

And with such delicate arguments I convince myself and a great deal of my countrymen that jumping queues has nothing to do with being a civilized or orderly society, especially when ours is the more successful (more numerous) species in the Darwinian sense. I may not be able to resist the temptation to jump queues, but can there be any doubt that I belong to a culture superior to the rest of the world?

Armed with such unimpeachable logic, I jump queues with the abandon of a kangaroo, even if I am not born the pushy sort – and truth be told, I belong to a race that is easily excitable, especially if the stakes are small enough. So robustly, ingeniously and earnestly – even if misguidedly – I chalk my queue-jumping trait to the account of our history of shortages, imagining it to be justification enough.

And with such justification I buttress my will for queue-jumping, without supplementing the will with a mastery of the nuances of the art.

For example, in the more nuanced art of queue-jumping, the trick is to delude the queue just as a honeybee deludes a flower by hiding its nefarious intent. What is more, a true queue-jumping ninja must jump a line with such finesse and feigned innocence that should an impractical victim object to his infraction, it is the objector who looks bad and not the maestro! Are we close to such elegance in matters of queue-jumping? Ask your conscience. As things stand, my fellow citizens and I appear crude and in-your-face in the way we jump queues – not subtle and nuanced. That is why I decided to write this book, hoping it would help us make up for such obvious deficiencies.

Queues: The God Illusion

Linked to patience or impatience is curiosity. Our curiosity as a people may not pitch us at the forefront of research-driven nations, but one can hardly quarrel with the postulate that we are a curious lot, especially when standing in queues. What is more, we have our own unique way of satiating that inquisitiveness. And I am not referring here to the guileless and probing questions that some of our countrymen casually ask of their co-queuers like: Where are you off to? Are you married? Do you have any *issues*? How many? What is your caste?

My allusion to curiosity was best described by a fellow student, Uday Menon, when I was a doctoral student at the Indian Institute of Management, Calcutta, over three decades ago (it wasn't Kolkata then). A stand-up comedy wizard, he once presented his take on Indian queues from the vantage point of the service provider sitting at the counter, facing a queue.

His take: a good Indian cannot simply stand relaxed in a queue twiddling his thumbs or reading a newspaper, as the Germans and the British seem to do. Every now and then, he has a compulsive need to crane his neck to the left or right, or to stand on his toes to glance over the heads of those ahead of him, to see what is going on further up front. Now, as the person at the counter takes in this view from his vantage point, he sees not only the face of the first person in the queue directly opposite him but also several other craniums sticking out virtually all around the head – to the left, right and above – of the foremost one, giving him the illusion that a revered Indian deity with multiple heads is standing before him.

To see this deity indulge in queue-jumping must be a spiritual experience unique to us.

We the Queue-jumping People

If there is one characteristic that binds the diverse nation together from Kashmir to Kanyakumari, it is the common propensity to jump queues. People of every caste, creed, language, state, religion, province and street – differ we may on virtually every other issue, but we all converge on this one ethos: the ethos of queue-jumping. We may have umpteen barriers that divide us – the rich from the poor; the literate from the illiterate; the urban from the rural; the haves from the have-nots; the English speakers from the non-English speakers. But there is no defined barrier that separates queue-jumpers from non-queue-jumpers as a category. The line dividing the two is as fuzzy as our queues. This is one fuzzy line, nay point, where the subcontinent stands more or less united, undivided, single-minded.

While freedom to jump queues is not formally enshrined in our Constitution as a fundamental right – a conspicuous omission no doubt on the part of our Constituent Assembly – it hardly prevents us from recognizing the right voluntarily, spontaneously and unerringly, and exercising it unabashedly. Except when we are physically restrained by a chain-link or flexi-fabric barrier or bamboo poles or cast iron pipes tightly lashed together with hemp ropes. Also, as citizens of a free nation, we have conferred upon ourselves this unwritten but fundamental and unassailable right: to be entirely self-absorbed with nary a care for the distress, discomfort or dismay of others.

This attitude is constantly nurtured, fertilized, cultivated and propagated from the cradle to the grave, in an ecosystem which has consistently failed to enforce appropriate and sufficient regulatory systems and processes for managing our queues in a civilized manner, and which is devoid of any penalty or fine for queue-jumping. As a consequence, if a system at all tries to enforce a fair queue, enough of us try our utmost to devise ways to thwart the system – with no mean success. Our native intelligence tells us that there is no downside in trying to jump a queue, and no profit in not doing so; and everybody is doing it anyway, so why shouldn't I? After all, this fatalistic stance – that everybody is doing it anyway – is also part of our ethos, culture and way of life as a people, and so we jump ahead of others who were clearly there in the line before us, without the slightest pang of guilt. Whether or not all of us actually jump queues, enough of us seem to do so to give the world the impression that queue-jumping is one of our national characteristics.

To derive maximum benefit from the book all that is required is that the readers be street-smart, reasonably flexible with their value system, not overly sensitive about taking advantage of a weak system and not easily embarrassed.

But first let us get an introduction to the sociological attitudes towards queues in different societies.

India Bashing?

Every now and then, Indian authors are accused of India-bashing. The typical motive ascribed is that 'India-bashing sells in the West'. Aravind Adiga's *The White Tiger* is mentioned as a case in point.

This theme came up a couple of weeks before this segment was being written, when I was attending someone's book release. The theme of the discussion was 'Indian fiction writing in English'. And sure enough, before long, the house was bashing authors for bashing India. The discussion touched a raw nerve in me, as I was also pilloried once as an India-basher on social media after an interview of mine on *Games Indians Play* was published by Knowledge@Wharton under the caption: 'Indians are privately smart and publicly dumb' – a line from the book.

So I asked the house some simple questions:

Can any Indian author – whether of fiction or non-fiction – when writing about India or a story set in India, forever steer clear of its humongous filth, open-air defecation, open drains, lack of sidewalks, its many unchecked diseases, messy traffic, interminable wait for delivery of justice, the VVIP culture, caste system, class system, the rotting jails, and the lives of the citizens lost in rain, sun, cold and draught and other such realities?

Can an author truthfully write a story involving a common man in India trying to build a house without telling the stories of the many corrupt agencies he has to negotiate to see his dream come true? Or a small businessman setting up a business likewise?

Can an author depict an average Indian woman in his novel as a protagonist without addressing the gender bias deeply ingrained in our culture?

Can an author tell the story of a generation without ever referring to the pandemic of bureaucratic apathy, or the rash of red tape, or the contagion of corruption that infest our regional transport offices, passport offices, land registration offices, or even the income tax offices where we have to go frequently?

Can an author honestly tell stories involving our politicians, with lips forever sealed against their parliamentary antics and the criminality that has become endemic in them? Or can the history of the Raj era be told honestly without telling the stories of our own petty squabbles, jealousies, infighting and bribery that facilitated their long rule in the subcontinent?

Can an author conscionably tell the story of a character in police custody without referring to how confessions are wrung out of him in the lock-up?

This is not to say there are no nice things or success stories in India worth telling. Of course, there are. And they do get told.

Walk into any bookshop and you will see some breathtaking images from virtually any of our states, our ancient and magnificent temples, palaces, caves, cave paintings, the rich flora and fauna and much else besides.

The whole of Bollywood and the other kinds of woods (whether Tolly, Molly, Kolly, Polly, or Golly) are dedicated to telling stories with happy endings.

Print and TV media are agog with leadership awards celebrating success stories in our industry, even if one may lament that the same bunch of aging names keeps cropping up over and over again for decades, and that the awards are covered abundantly in the very newspapers or channels that were the sponsors of the event.

And just in case some good stories are unwittingly left out, there are enough good nationalists constantly reminding us that we have a 5,000-year-old rich culture; that there is nothing happening in today's world that we didn't already do or know of 2,000 or maybe 4,000 years ago; that we are without doubt a culture superior to the West because, in our understanding, Western culture starts and ends with kissing in public.

There is no dearth of instances where we celebrate our successes. So why are we so touchy about occasional instances of 'India-bashing', especially when we could hugely benefit from a good kick on our collective backside for our many wayward ways which bring the nation little respect of the world at large?

I underscored in the said gathering that, as I saw it, our glorious past can hardly be a consolation for our sorry present.

I am glad to say that those at the gathering saw my point.

It seems to me that in India the sin lies not in one's shameful conduct but in being caught in the act, or worse, accepting the wrongdoing, or, even worse, pointing it out glaringly. As long as we have not confessed to the wrong conduct, we can strut around like nothing wrong ever happened. Likewise, our tragedy lies not in being the way we are but only in our portraying it thus. And then we bash some folks for being India bashers and, that done, imagine all is kosher about India.

If queue-jumping were our only major shortcoming as a people, perhaps we would not need to be too apologetic. All the people in the world have their share of pimples and pustules, and we would have ours. Nor is queue-jumping peculiar only to us as a people, as we shall see in the next chapter. Unless we are ready to face our defects, we shall forever remain fearful of looking at ourselves in the mirror. If we wish to be beautiful and to present our best face to the world, we will have to work on our abundance of warts and moles.

2

The Sociology of Queues across Nations

An Indian dies and goes to hell. There he finds that each country has a separate hell and one may opt to sign up for any of them.

He goes first to the German hell and asks, 'What do they do here?' He is told, 'First they put you in an electric chair for an hour. Then they lay you on a bed of nails for another hour. Then the German devil comes in and whips you for the rest of the day.' The man does not like the sound of it at all, and so he moves on to the American hell. Here too he is told the same routine: 'First they put you in an electric chair for an hour. Then they lay you on a bed of nails for another hour. Then the American devil comes in and whips you for the rest of the day.' He then tries a few other hells and gets the same answer to his question.

Then finally he comes to the Indian hell and finds that there is a very long queue of people waiting to get in. Amazed, he asks, 'What do they do here?' And to his surprise, once again he receives the same answer.

He exclaims, 'What the hell! That's exactly the same as all the other hells – so what's the long queue for?'

He receives the response: 'Because maintenance is so bad, the electric chair does not work, someone has stolen all the nails from the bed, and the devil is a former Government of India babu. So he comes in, signs the register and then goes off to the cafeteria...'

In an ideal world, there should be no queues. It may be argued that queues inherently represent inefficiencies in the functioning of a market. In the utopia of economists, there is little place for queues. In testimony to the fact that we live in a less-than-ideal world, queues exist, and utopias don't. And where queues do exist, they are also great equalizers, at least in many democratic societies. They represent egalitarianism. So what are the attitudes to queues and queue-jumping across nations – capitalist and socialist states alike?

Queuing Attitudes: China versus India

While to the uninitiated Westerner both Indian and Chinese queues may appear equally boorish, the truth is there is a clear difference between the two.

Anecdotal wisdom has it that the Chinese have a visceral dislike for queues and simply *refuse* to form lines, except when faced with the barrel of a gun. Also, according to Professor Shi-mian, they are honest and upfront about it and show their disdain for queues by simply refusing to form them.[1]

We, on the other hand, would like to convince ourselves that we are in favour of queues – as long as we are at the head of them. If we are not, we start jumping them as soon as we form them. This is not unlike what we do when outside an overcrowded train compartment. We do everything in our power to get in, but no sooner do we find ourselves inside than we start preventing others from entering.

Which of the two – Chinese or Indian attitude – one finds more infuriating depends on one's situation, choice and sense of nationalism.

Others may hold the opinion that the line which divides the two attitudes is in fact blurry. For example, the news report in China Daily Show also refers to an interesting experiment conducted at Tsinghua University in 1994, which reinforces the standard hypothesis that the Chinese simply refuse to form queues.[2] The 'bus experiment' involved asking a dozen students to remain in single file as a bus driven by the researchers pulled up. The researchers gathered ample evidence in support of their hypothesis as they observed the twelve students push, jostle and trample over each other to get on board the vehicle. That the bus was visibly empty and had plenty of seating space didn't seem to matter. While these researchers in their wisdom may not have conducted an identical experiment in India, which one of us would shy away from betting a rupee that had they done so, they would not have seen identical results? So who can vouch in all honesty that the Tsinghua University scene is not quite representative of any of our own Indian bus stops, even the ones in Mumbai, where only a few decades ago forming queues at bus stops was not uncommon. Ah, nostalgia!

Queuing in Singapore: As Expected

Queuing attitudes in South Asia more or less mimic India's, while those in much of South-East Asia mimic China's. Singaporeans, though primarily comprising Chinese, Malays and Indians – none of whom are the world's greatest queuers – have collectively developed a unique ethos and culture for their queues. Singaporean Timothy Tang writes in a blog that as citizens his countrymen have become so competitive that they will be willing to queue overnight just to be the first in line for any freebie or trivial knick-knack – say, a robotic toy. Their social media often mocks those who line up thus, pejoratively referring to them as 'kiasu' – greedy and superficial.[3] And, of course, true to Singapore's typical response to such 'chaos', which they consider a shame given their love for elegant and proper systems, they have taken to offering a special online service that caters to the demands of the 'kiasu' so that there would be no kiasus any more!

Queuing Down Under: Not Topsy-turvy in the Least

In Australia and neighbouring New Zealand, queuing is the default setting, whether for buses, trains or cabs. Government agencies, too, take queue management seriously. Take the Australian Government Medicare for example. The organization is committed to continuous improvement in customer service, believing in the need to operate effectively at every point of customer service, and is not shy of deploying emerging technologies towards this end. Not long ago I observed a public request for a tender, issued by Medicare Australia, looking for a supplier to provide a turnkey queuing solution: installation of and support for an automated queuing system across their network of Medicare offices.[4] So a friendly warning: the next time you are down under, mess with their queues only if you have mastered this book first.

Queuing Japanese Style: Tailored to Precision

After Seiri, Seiton, Seiso, Seiketsu, Shitsuke (the 5-S Japanese housekeeping system) and what have you, you would expect queuing is the natural state of Japan. Come rain, chill or snow, the integrity of queues is inviolate. Whether for a pack of takoyaki (octopus dumpling), or while waiting at a pachinko (parlour) for a new video game, or at an autograph-signing session with an idol, the Japanese will queue. Period. But you can expect the Japanese to do anything to perfection. What is the single biggest downside of standing in a queue? Waste of time, right? Well, the Japanese have more or less solved that problem. I saw a YouTube clipping not long ago that shows fans overcoming the problem of lining up from the previous night for their favourite game at a large stadium.[5] They just came, wrote down their names on the ground outside the gates in the sequence of their arrival, and left. They returned a couple of hours before the game, just as the gates were opening, to simply walk in and occupy their seats. Now if you think they defaced the ground with all the markings, well, you have got Japan figured out all wrong. No, they merely stuck tapes on the ground and wrote their names and order of arrival on those!

Something akin to this is also seen in India, often in front of municipal taps, in the form of assorted pots and pans of plastic and metal. The municipalities in their infinite wisdom release potable water to the populace at ungodly hours, like 4 a.m. On such occasions, rather than queue up so early in the streets, people simply place their vessels as their surrogates in the queues overnight and make an appearance just as the water is released. But, alas, these means are not always respected – quarrels and fights at taps are a common sight.

Queuing in Britain: Alternative Religion

One would like to bet that everyone must hate queues, except when one is at the head of the line. But one may lose the bet. Popular wisdom tells us that the British, specifically the Caucasian British, love their queues so much that they line up for virtually everything, to the point where, it is said, if an Englishman were left alone, he would form a queue of one. It may be said that a man in a queue is as much a cultural symbol of Britain as a matador is of Spain and a cowboy is of Texas. Or a queue-jumper is of India.

British versus Indian Attitudes to Queuing

The English like their queues orderly and neat, while we love ours – when we form them, that is – chaotic and messy. For the English, queue-jumping is only a slightly lesser offence than violation of one's human rights, while for us, *it is* our human right.

Just watch a debate on BBC, with everyone politely awaiting their turn to speak, and compare it to the daily shouting matches on our prime-time television, with up to ten speakers and the anchor trying to speak simultaneously, and you will appreciate the difference. For British nationals, queuing is a fine and elegant art, just as queue-jumping is a highly honed and practised art form for us. The British propensity for queuing is equalled (or is it surpassed?) only by the Germans. Ralf Dahrendorf, a German who once headed the venerable London School of Economics, went so far as to say, 'I have a feeling that this island is uninhabitable, and therefore people have tried to make it habitable by being reasonable with one another.'[6] The German had thus accredited the British queuing practices and in the same sentence summed up the German attitude to queues as well.

Of course, there are those who claim that even the British patience with queues might be wearing thin after all and that they are no longer as prim about queuing up as they once were. Maybe they are slowly but surely giving in to the entropy doctrine, or at least to their South Asian diaspora?

Little wonder that the South Asian often stands out in the United Kingdom when it comes to attitudes towards queue-jumping, notwithstanding historical British attempts to get us to queue up. It is said that in the mid-eighteenth century, Robert Clive – the then commander-in-chief of British India – did his earnest best to get Calcuttans to queue up. And rumours abound that the general Indian propensity to fob off queues notwithstanding, the Calcuttans have retained some of that learning to this day.

Chinese versus British Outlook to Queues

And what happens when the Chinese and British cultures intersect, you may wonder. For an answer, we just have to look at Hong Kong. Interestingly, we are told the social codes in colonial Hong Kong in the 1960s were more Chinese than British. In any queue, the cue to success was brute force and not social order. Apparently, it was the American McDonald's that brought the queuing culture to the then island state. When it opened shop in the mid-1970s, the cash registers were faced with crowds of people hollering orders and brandishing money over the heads of those in front of them. McDonald's deployed young women to streamline the crowds, and ever since orderly queues have been a hallmark of the island, their Chinese roots notwithstanding.[7] Well, clearly, strange things do happen. We can only pray that someone brings about a similar volte-face in our culture as well.

Queuing in Europe: Elegant as Most Things European

One may also quibble over whether the English or the Germans actually *like* queues or merely *tolerate* them but nevertheless do it right. Wherever their predilection for queues may stem from, the result is more or less the same – a disciplined queue wherever you look. Also, there is another thing common between the English and the Germans: both are a reserved and reticent lot. But try breaking their queues and you would have seriously messed with their sensibilities and inflamed their sensitive side.

The Swedes, prefer a high degree of orderliness, with

an allotted number on a ticket. Here, and in neighbouring Norway (and also most places in Switzerland, it would seem), you take a ticket even if you are in a queue of one. The Portuguese for some reason have the same proclivity. They have machines dispensing *sneha* (tickets) all over, and you barely enter a place before you encounter one. A man may survive a day without the euro, but not without *sneha*. Consequently, in these nations, queues are not as restricting as they are in many other parts of the world, for you can easily go in and out of the vicinity as long as you are there when your turn comes.

The Dutch are relatively bad queuers, with decreasing tolerance for queues – but only by British standards, not ours. For example, according to author and travel writer Rodney Bolt, queueing among the Dutch is an '… abstract affair. On entering a shop, the Dutch make a mental note of who was there before them. The shop assistants abnegate all responsibility, simply by calling out "Who's next?", leaving it to the customers to assert their rights of precedence, which they do in no uncertain terms.'[8]

The Italians for the most part do queue up, albeit with a bit of fluidity. Occasional line-jumping is not unknown, but it is usually accomplished with typical Italian flair. For example, says *Italy Magazine*, 'Apparently if you queue once, pay but then forget to buy something, you have the right to leave your shopping bags at the till, go back into the supermarket, get what you forgot, jump the queue with almost ten people waiting, pay and happily go home.'[9]

Spain (and Cuba) follow somewhat different protocols,

and do not necessarily form perceptible queues. It is not unusual in these countries for a person arriving at an ice cream parlour or a bus stop, for instance, to ask, 'Quién es el último?' or 'Who is the last?' and then 'stand' around that individual, even though the 'standing' is not quite one behind the other but a seemingly random assortment of people with the same expectation of service.

Queuing in the Soviet Union: More about Shortages than Sociology

In the former Soviet Union countries, including much of Eastern Europe, long queues, even for daily bread, were a common enough sight. It can be easily seen that in controlled economies, the long queues are a proxy for supressed inflation. The relationship between inflation and queues needs some elaboration.

In reasonably free markets, most of us intuitively understand what inflation means. We experience inflation when prices of most goods and services we consume go up. The more they go up, the higher we believe inflation to be and vice versa.

But exactly why do prices of goods and services produced and sold in an economy go up in the first place? It may happen for any one or a combination of three reasons. One, when people start spending faster than producers can supply goods and services; two, when there is scarcity of goods and services in the economy; and three, when the amount of currency in circulation is very high compared to the value of goods and services in the system.

Inflation in a system can manifest itself only when prices are allowed to reflect the demand-supply gap of goods and services. Such a system is usually known as a free market system. As economies liberalize, with government control on prices lifted, prices of goods, which in a centralized regime were always in short supply, begin to rise, because demand continues to exceed supply. And as this gap increases, prices are allowed to increase in sympathy. There are fewer people who can afford the higher prices. The length of the queues does not necessarily increase much, though the affordability of the goods and supplies goes down.

However, in centralized or controlled regimes like the Soviet Union, the government would invariably be averse to allowing price increases. But demand perennially outstrips supply for a variety of reasons – corruption, centralization of decision making, narrow spans of control, or lack of entrepreneurship being some of them. The inflation inherent in the economy is artificially repressed by these regimes, resulting in longer queues.

Longer queues become a proxy for high inflation. You can appreciate why queues in some of these economies had to be long when you consider the hyperinflation in the early-twentieth century, which raged at millions of percentage points (as against the 5 to 6 percentage-point inflation currently in India)! For example, such was the hyperinflation in East Germany in the 1920s that the mark-dollar exchange rate rose from 4.2 to 1 dollar in 1914 to 4.2 trillion to 1 dollar in 1923, forcing the government's Reichsbank to issue a banknote with a face value of 100

trillion mark (100,000,000,000,000; or 100 million million)![10]
If you are stunned by that figure, well, you are being hasty.
A quarter of a century later, in the immediate aftermath of
the Second World War, Hungary's inflation got to a point
where the Hungarian National Bank ended up issuing
banknotes of the highest ever denomination: 100 quintillion
pengo (100,000,000,000,000,000,000, or 10^{20}, or 100 million
million million)![11] In Greece, inflation in 1944 had reached
8.5 billion per cent; in Republika Srpska, a breakaway
region of Bosnia, formerly of Yugoslavia, the inflation rate
in 1994 was 297 million per cent.[12] One can give scores of
such shocking statistics from all over the world. But the
point of these numbers is that when inflation runs so high,
a banknote is merely reduced to a piece of paper that cannot
buy anything because the supply of goods has simply dried
up in the economy. What it really means is that goods are
in extremely scarce supply, and hence the queues run really
long.

As a consequence of long queues that have prevailed
in the centralized economies for a century, the code of
conduct associated with queuing and queue-jumping in
these countries became much more institutionalized and
is much more regulated to this day. In Russia, for instance,
queuing has developed into nuanced etiquette as a result of
years of stagnation. However, even as things have improved
in these countries, the younger generation often views the
older ones, brought up on the long queues of yesteryears,
as a trifle pushy and are said to be wary of the old ladies
who may push their way to the head of a queue in the blink
of an eye.

An excellent commentary on these protocols can be seen in the hilarious pre-glasnost and pre-perestroika novel *The Queue* by Vladimir Sorokin (see box below). According to Sorokin, the era of Joseph Stalin (1922-1953) turned the entire Soviet Union into one gigantic 'line of lines', and later, as if in a collective ode to the deceased leader, the 'masses dissolved into obedient molecules', turning into 'tranquil masses'.[13] The time of Nikita Khrushchev (1958-1964) saw the ritual of standing in queues acquiring its 'definitive features, having cleansed itself of arbitrary individualism'.[14] And by the reign of Leonid Brezhnev (1964-1982), queues had become a hallmark of established socialism and acquired an honoured place alongside such other profound symbols as St Basil's Cathedral, Russian Caviar, the Russian Revolution, Lenin's mausoleum and the Soviet military threat.

The Queue was originally published in Russian as *Ochered* and first published in English in 1988. In *The Queue*, Sorokin takes the reader through the archetypal Russian institution of queues, with all the irony and humour that the author can muster. Such is the setting and the presentation of the novel that the readers come to identify themselves with the situation described and experience all the travails, trauma and tease of standing in the line. The work revolves around the protagonists Vadim and Lena. Vadim is waiting in a serpentine line where nobody quite seems to know what they are in line for (like the situation in *The Trial* – by Franz

Kafka – in which the protagonist, Joseph K, a bank officer, is unexpectedly arrested one fine morning, but nobody has an idea for what). The queue itself is presented not by description but through a rendition of the cacophony of voices typical of a queue, complete with snatches of conversations, wisecracks and spontaneous humour of the situation. It is in this queue that Vadim meets the other protagonist, Lena.

À la the queues for Apple's latest products today, at the end of the day, the queuers find that they will have to return to the queue the next morning to receive whatever it is they are in the queue for. Lena takes it upon herself to bring more order to the queue and starts distributing tokens to the queuers. At the end of the day, Vadim and Lena decide to spend the night on some park benches along with other queuers. The same scene as the day before plays out all over again the next day, with most still having no clue what the queue is for, or trying to estimate the prices of whatever it is that is being sold. Some try to speculate upon the rate at which the queue is being serviced. The entire sociology of a Russian queue of the period is played out eminently, with queuers shown to be taking small breaks from time to time to go to the restrooms or for some quick refreshments and so forth – in effect, joining some other queues! Someone decides to make another check of those still in the queue. At last, after two days, the end of the queue is in sight, but then it starts raining. At this point, Vadim takes shelter in an adjoining building; in one of those apartments lives a lady by the name of Lyuda. She invites him to her apartment and serves him a simple but welcoming meal. She proves to be an engaging conversationalist, and one thing leads to another and the two end up making love and fall asleep for the night. In the morning Vadim discovers that Lyuda works at the store outside which he and everyone else was queued up and discovers that his days of waiting in the queue were entirely wasted because he could easily have used the good offices of Lyuda to jump the long queue.

No wonder today there are standard commonly accepted protocols for queues in the former Soviet Union countries, which provide social protection to queuers against queue-jumping. For example, one may take time out from a queue to use the restroom, or even get a quick haircut (or other such short diversions) and then return to one's original place in the line without much ado or without being viewed as a queue-jumper. It is also acceptable for one to jump a queue for urgent reasons, such as purchasing a ticket for an immediately departing bus or train. There are other minor nuances. For example, East Europeans usually prefer to queue up sideways, say, against a wall (probably a remnant from the days of having to rest your back while standing in long queues), while in the US, for instance, they prefer to queue up directly opposite the service counter.

Queuing in the US: Queuing?

Americans and queues? Well, until recently, they simply did not queue up. They only lined up; and that too not often, living in the land of plenty as they do. Except maybe for the latest Apple products. With their flair for technology, the Americans have devised plenty of 'queue management systems' to keep their lines in check. What is more, if there are any queue-jumpers at all, they are probably scared of being sued, and so the queue-jumping propensity is largely unknown. Except maybe in the movie halls in the city of New York where everyone rushes in pell-mell as soon as the doors open. This, of course, offers a level playing field to non-resident Indians and persons of Indian origin alike, who are hardly strangers to such propensity. Our countrymen, we are told, are second to none in slithering in smoothly as the crowd is let in, ending up with the choicest seats.

Nevertheless queues have been serious enough business for the Americans to undertake deep research and come up with appropriate regulations and systems. For instance, legislators in the state of Washington have enacted a bill that makes cutting a line or queue-jumping when catching a ferry illegal, with a fine of $101, apart from being forced to return to the end of the line.

Inexplicably, some recent trends indicate that the Americans are beginning to use the Q-word more and more, thanks mainly to Netflix. Netflix, with tens of millions of members who trawl the ether for movies and TV soaps, is increasingly using 'queues' to describe the line-up of videos. But whether they queue up or line up, much of the formal research in the field of queuing is done in the land of the Americans.

Queuing in Africa: With Apology

Africa is a big continent and any generalization may be unfair. But the observations of George Ayittey, a distinguished Ghanaian economist, author and academic who has served at several American universities, come very close. He says that elections are the one time Africans take their queues seriously.[15] They rise early to queue up patiently for hours under the hot sun and make a gala event of it. However, God save the misguided soul who tries to pinch another's place in the voting line. One might as well try and purloin a lion's kill from its jaws.

Indian versus Western Queues

How do our attitudes to queues fare vis-à-vis Western ones?[16] Western queues, for the most part, are products of modern principles of egalitarian democracy, so that they ignore power, privilege and wealth and follow the 'first come, first served' (FCFS) system – a system which is considered fair and democratic, treating all people as equal so that they are served in the order of their arrival. Of course, we all recognize that both in the West and in our own country, it is not as if FCFS is the only correct criteria for resource allocation under all situations. There are any number of situations where this rule does not apply, and quite rightly so. For example, few universities and colleges worldwide give admissions or scholarships on the basis of FCFS. The rule usually applied is that of merit. In other contexts, we use need (as in medical emergency), or even chance or lottery (as in allocation of municipal plots), as the more appropriate criteria for allocating resources.

However, our subject of focus here is largely social queues, as we conventionally recognize them. It is in this context that the West regards FCFS as a largely fair and the most egalitarian criteria in most social situations. They practically regard a fair queue to be the loadstone of order, organization, the equity of a system and equality of people. Apart from fairness, the FCFS principle also represents concern for others – a way to show that we respect others' time as much as we do our own. To the average Westerner, the FCFS principle represents a sense of right, and queue-jumping a sense of wrong. For them, joining and holding one's legitimate place in a queue is nearly a spiritual thing, or at least an unselfish act – sacrificing one's time so that society functions reliably, amicably and predictably. In their scheme of things, a queue-jumper causes the collapse of this order and predictability and contributes to chaos and collapse of order in the community.

As if to reinforce this point, about the time this chapter was being written (July 2014), President Barack Obama of the US was in the news for 'queue-jumping', though it was not the type you and I ordinarily indulge in. Apparently, the affable president had stepped into Franklin's, a reputed barbecue restaurant in Texas, for a quick bite. The wait in the line for food there is known to extend up to two to three hours. But the president, in a bit of a hurry, put to use some of the prerogatives of his office and jumped the queue. He offered to buy the family he was jumping ahead of their lunch. Bruce Finstad of Houston, the shrewd man whose family the president had offered to buy lunch for, wasn't the kind to let go of a free meal and a chance to deliver a good lesson. He ordered some three pounds of beef, two pounds of ribs, a half pound of turkey and an equal measure of sausage, landing a shocked Obama with a $300 cheque, inclusive of the president's own lunch and that of his staff.

Americans being Americans, by next afternoon, the restaurant was running a poll asking the world (meaning America) at large whether Obama should have cut the line. Fortunately for Obama, of the 200 folks polled, 145 'liked' the president jumping the queue, while only fifty-five were unhappy, saying he should have waited his turn. That's the West in general and the wild west of Texas in particular for you.

In July 2012, Prime Minister David Cameron of the UK was chided crisply by a waitress for jumping a queue, with, 'I am in the middle of serving somebody!' Then she made him wait ten minutes for a coffee. The good PM was returning from the Armed Forces Day in Plymouth on a Saturday morning, preoccupied with the burdens of the world, when he decided to make a quick dash into the Sandwich Box Plus Café, perhaps as much for a coffee as for the politician's need for being seen to be socializing. Sheila Thomas, busy behind the counter, did not recognize Cameron and that is when she displayed her visceral British dislike for queue-jumping to none other than the PM.

We can never ever catch the Indian president, or the prime minister, or even a lowly chief minister, jumping a queue in the crass fashion of President Obama. That is because by the time the roads are cleared by half the police force of the state and the restaurant is emptied by the Special Protection Group, or even the lesser Z+ category personnel with their sniffer dogs sniffing everything including probably the food in the kitchen, there is no queue left to jump.

So when it comes to queuing, Westerners and Indians are as different as chalk and cheese. In any case, Western queues are mostly a lifeless, boring and linear assortment of people standing somberly, as if struck by life's most extreme tragedy. Not so ours. Our average queues are full of verve and vitality, each brain in overdrive, actively evaluating all strategies to jump the queue. What is more, in our queues we stand really tight, unlike the Westerners, who stand apart as if the next person may be suffering from some unmentionable contagion. That is why our queues, when they exist at all, are a solid, albeit uneven, line of people with all senses on alert, rather than the relaxed and limp lines seen in the West.

Even when it comes to cars in the Western world, you would notice that they follow a lane in perfect alignment, one behind the other, spaced equally and amply. Not us. No way. We never follow the unnecessary constraints of lanes to inhibit our style and always move bumper-to-bumper, lest a Maruti 800 and half a dozen two-wheelers wedge themselves between our car and the one ahead. Just as one side of our brain is constantly devising ways to jump the queue, the other side works out a strategy to leave no gaps in the queue unsealed. That is also probably why no part of our brains takes serious offence at the queue-jumpers, as we are all doing it.

No wonder we present a major headache to countries like the UK, for instance, into which our thronging expatriates are forever trying to meld, like oil in water.

With the sociology of queues behind us, let me move on to their physiology in the next chapter.

3

The Physiology of Queues

I was in a queue at the supermarket when I noticed a rather attractive young lady behind me waving out to me.

I was rather taken aback, and although her face was vaguely familiar, I couldn't place where I might have known her from, and so I said, 'Sorry, do we know each other?'

She replied, 'I may be mistaken, but I thought you might be the father of one of my children.'

Sweat broke out on my temples, and my mind reeled back to the one and only time I had been unfaithful to my wife. 'Don't tell me!' I exclaimed, 'Wasn't it on the Goa beach just off the Pausada Hotel that we met?' And I continued, 'I swear, when I was released from the police station and got back to the hotel room, you had left.'

'What are you talking about?' she replied. 'I'm your son's English teacher.'

History, geography, sociology and anthropology of queues and queue-jumping are all very well, but it is now time to take a look at the physiology of queues a little more closely and systematically. Defining a queue, even if we are not the model queuers of the world, is easy, even without resorting to the Webster or the OED. Here is my definition: A queue is a line or sequence of service seekers awaiting their turn to be attended to or to proceed through.

A queue may be a formal or a social system. But in either case, the FCFS principle is usually implied, while cutting in or violating it is considered a deviation from the norm.

Also, queues can be formal, social, real, virtual, overt or covert and may present any number of other variants in between.

Formal Queues

Formal queues are those which are formed because the managerial system demands it. For example, in a bank, the teller would usually operate strictly on an FCFS principle. Often the systems are made even more formal by awarding a token number to the service seeker and ensuring that the service is provide strictly according to the number awarded.

Social Queues

Queues which are not formally supervised or enforced are generally social queues. The queues at bus stops, municipal taps, taxi stands, grocery stores, pharmacies, cricket grounds and so on are all mostly social queues. These queues also aspire to follow the FCFS system, even if in a miraculous show of unity, the entire nation comes together to snuff out that aspiration.

Semi-formal Queues

These are obviously the queues that fall somewhere between formal and social queues. Airport entry gates, restaurants, or even malls often maintain semi-formal queues

Real Queues

Real queues are ones where people can actually be seen standing in a line. For example, lines at bus stops, taxi stands, cinema halls, ration shops, lifts, airport security counters, ticketing counters, boarding gates, RTO offices and pretty much most queues around us are typically real queues. Historically, our populous nation with its sluggish economic growth provided a plethora of opportunities for real queues to form. Our 9 per cent growth era brought about some changes, no doubt – from waiting for years for telephone connections, we now wait only a few months for a passport – a situation slowly changing for the better.

We can identify two kinds of real queues, namely Real Real-Queues and Virtual Real-Queues.

Real Real-Queues (or RRQs) answer to the same definition that we used for Real Queues above, namely, lines where you can actually see real people lined up. These are the most common queues.

The Virtual Real-Queues (or VRQs) are the ones where objects substitute people, but otherwise the queues are as good as real. The queues in front of municipal taps in the form of pots and pans that we referred to in the previous chapter may be considered VRQs. These pots and pans represent the position of people in the queue. Even when we step out of RRQs, we leave behind a briefcase, a book or a slipper to indicate that we have not surrendered our place. In this sense, a VRQ is merely an extreme case of the RRQ in which nearly every member of the line is represented by an object.

Virtual Queues

Virtual queues are queues where you do not actually see people or even objects lined up physically, but they are lined up for service or admittance nevertheless. There are three categories of virtual queues one can think of.

1. Virtual queues of the first kind (or VQ1), where people are not lined up in person but waitlisted in sequence towards some common objective. The objective of the waiting list could be, say, allocation of housing; admission in a well-known educational institution; admittance of patients in a high-end government or private hospital; allocation of a railway berth; or allotment of choicest municipal plots, shops, gas agencies and so on.
2. Virtual queues of the second kind (or VQ2) are what we witness in banks or passport offices, for example, where people are issued a sequence number upon arrival and then the number is called either on an electronic board or hollered out sequentially by the service provider. People may or may not be physically present around the service location. It doesn't matter as long as they answer when their allotted number is called.

3. Virtual queues of the third kind (or VQ3) are those formed over the phone, as in for reserving a table at a restaurant or for an appointment at the hairdresser's or the dentist's.

Overt, Covert, Explicit and Implicit Queues

Most queues we come across, whether real or virtual, are overt or explicit. But queues don't always have to be overt. They can be covert as well. Take for example the deplaning of passengers from an aircraft. It is implicitly expected that those seated in front of us will deplane before us, even though there is no queue as such. Fairness and civility, where these things are meaningful, may demand that if we are in row 6, we will wait for those in row 5 to deplane before us. This is an implicit queue. Another example of a covert queue is when a staffer at an airline's boarding gate announces that the aged, women with children or a certain set of rows should board ahead of other passengers. Covert queues are virtually non-queues as far as we as a people are concerned, for we seldom even respond to even explicit requests or announcements, leave alone to tacit expectations.

Approximate Queues

Almost all queues in our land are approximate queues.

Let me explain how I queue. Given my innate proclivity for jumping lines, and a nation full of others like me, it is a puzzle how our social queues get formed at all in the first place. It is as if Dr Jekyll in my heart tells me that orderly queues are a necessity for the functioning of a civilized society. But just as my heart begins to follow his voice, Mr Hyde in my mind takes over and questions the former's naïve call to suffer the queue when there is a significant reward – in terms of time saved or competitive spirit satiated – to be reaped by jumping it, and there is no downside whatsoever – no penalty, not even a social sanction – for attempting the jump. So it is of course a rational and smart move to try and jump the queue. But if trying to jump a queue is the smart thing to do for me, it is equally the smart thing to do for my 1.3 billion compatriots. As a consequence, our queues have that fluid, cloud-like quality of constantly changing form in a delicate tug-of-war between our hearts and our minds. And as a result what we have are these approximate queues, just as we drive approximately to the left of the road or have approximate sidewalks or approximately full convertibility of the rupee – very Indian, very 'us', very identifiable, just as any other product made in India is immediately identifiable as Made in India for its approximate finish.

Randomized Queues

There are systems in which people are waiting to be serviced but their place in the queue is randomized, as, for example, when I wait at a baggage carousel at an airport, not knowing when my bag is going to turn up. But even such 'random queues' do not usually dissuade me from queue-jumping. For instance, I look around keenly for someone who has unwittingly allowed a gap of more than six inches betwixt himself and the carousel, and no sooner do I spot such folly than I wedge myself in that wee fissure to be ahead of the simpleton who made the mistake, and I make sure he stays behind me until my bag appears.

Even otherwise, waiting in such random queues can be most frustrating, because one is so close to the destination and yet held up somewhat indefinitely. The impatience of indefinite waiting manifests itself in much irritability giving us our licence to jump queues.

When Random Queues are Distasteful

The *New York Times* reported an episode where a Houston airport received several complaints from travellers about the inordinate wait at some specific carousels for bags.[1] Customary solutions such as increasing the number of baggage handlers for the shift and closer coordination did reduce the waiting time but not the customer complaints. What puzzled the investigators was that the average waiting time at these carousels was not significantly higher than that at the other carousels.

A closer scrutiny of the site revealed that the walk between the arrival gate and the baggage claim area was about a minute, while the average waiting time for baggage at most carousels, including the ones in question which were closest to the arrival gates, was about seven minutes. So, at the carousels nearest to the arrival gates nearly 88 per cent of the total time between deplaning and collection of bags was spent waiting! For the more distant carousels, this was not the case. So the airport authorities merely shifted the main arrival gate and the carousels in question in such a way as to increase the distance between them. With these measures, the complaints stopped! Clearly, the mere act of waiting is distasteful.

Where There Is a Queue, There Is Queue-jumping

Where there are queues, queue-jumping cannot be far away; at least not east of the Indus, where the two live cheek by jowl. Other words for queue-jumping are barging, breaking, budding, budging, bumping, butting, ditching, pushing, shorting and skipping – all of which stand for the act of entering a line at any position other than the tail end, violating the norm of FCFS.

Is queue-jumping essentially limited to social queues alone? Or is the incidence of queue-jumping necessarily hierarchical, in the sense that formal queues are the hardest to jump, followed by semi-formal ones, followed by social ones?

'Not necessarily,' is my answer to both questions.

In social queues, which are for a time-bound event or rationed products, queue-jumping can get quite hard. People in such queues are far more aggressive and far less tolerant of queue-jumpers. For example, at municipal taps queue-jumping is fiercely prohibited and any attempt to jump is rebutted determinedly. In this sense, though these are social queues, they are difficult to jump, and that too at great risk to life and limb. In such cases, discretion is the better part of valour.

On the other hand, even in formal or semi-formal systems, it is not uncommon for the managers themselves to allow for the violation of the FCFS principle, like when a doctor places a board outside his clinic asking people to allow emergency cases to jump the line; or when airline staff routinely escort those whose flight is about to depart ahead of others who are not in an equal hurry (though this does not happen as often at airports in other parts of the world).

And then we have those serving the counters who could well be my partners in cheating the waiting public. Here my queue-jumping may be a tad more nuanced but not absent. Instead of jumping bodily, if I have any clout, I manage to send one of the office attendants directly behind the ticketing or check-in counter so that my job is done behind the scenes, unknown to those in the queue, who naively assume that the service time has somehow gone up.

General Determinants of Queue-jumping Propensity (QJP)

Different kinds of queues enable, empower or encourage queue-jumping to different degrees and in different ways. This is important for any dedicated and aspiring queue-jumper to understand. And to be able to do that one must understand the many physiognomies of queues which inspire or inhibit queue-jumping behaviour. This will ensure that one jumps queues more intelligently and with a greater degree of success.

Let us consider an example of a Real Queue from each of its two sub-categories: an RRQ outside a ration shop and a VRQ of pots and pans in front of a municipal tap. On average, those forming both these queues may statistically be from the less privileged sections of society, in terms of education and wealth. However, these queues on average seem to work with considerable efficiency, with QJP being less pervasive, or, when attempted, being severely discouraged by peer pressure – the deterrent usually handed out on the spot by the other queuers in no uncertain terms. Thus, these queues are often reasonably well-defined and even disciplined. In such queues, one is safest reining in one's natural urge to jump the queue.

Education and Wealth

One may be inclined to associate QJP with lack of sophisticated education. If that's your hypothesis, well, you have your black swan. The fact is that QJP is much more rampant in RRQs at airports, where the constituents are largely from the more educated and wealthier categories, than those at municipal taps or ration shops. With little or virtually no disincentive or deterrence to QJP, attempts to jump queues at, say, security screening, are way more ubiquitous. This is because when one jumps the queue in front of you, you have two alternatives. Stay quiet and do nothing, or protest firmly. In the first case, you allow the aggressor to succeed in his mission and he is incentivized by your silence. In the second case, when you protest firmly, you run the risk of appearing churlish, as your objection may appear disproportionately stern or aggressive when the sophisticated aggressor's ploy was rather casual and nuanced, calculated to make your remonstration appear like an overreaction. All the aggressor has to do when challenged is to give you your comeuppance, for example, by looking surprised and telling you very politely not to get worked up – with a 'Chill, dude' kind of look – given that 'all of us are going to catch our flights anyway'. Now you look foolish, especially as no one else seems to be at all concerned or coming to your support, because the onus of such a challenge is usually on the bloke ahead of whom the queue-jumping happens – meaning, you. This is a ploy that usually works very well

The lesson here is clear. Queue-jumping in our part of the world seems to have little to do with education or wealth. In fact, the greater the wealth, the higher the sense of entitlement with which the queue-jumping is done. Mostly, it is about whether or not I think I will get away with it. So when I think I can get away with it, it is well worth my while to attempt the jump.

I must add here that there is something about airports that seems to stimulate every queue-jumping hormone in my body. Even as I am approaching the terminal and see a queue forming for identification before entry into the terminal building, my steps quicken, as if of their own volition, to overtake that old gentleman who is himself doing his best to hasten his strides, keeping me at the corner of his cornea, so to speak, to beat me to the security entrance! If I can outpace him before he reaches the queue, I can hardly be labelled a queue-jumper in letter. The spirit is irrelevant, in any case, in our scheme of things. So I strive a tad harder, without making my effort so obvious that it looks patently vulgar; but at a pinch, I let even that fig leaf of politeness drop. It is the same when a flight is announced – when I try to jump both explicit and implicit queues. I ignore explicit queues when I deliberately form a second or a third line, knowing fully well where the tail of the original line is. I jump the implicit queue when I ignore the repeated calls of the airline staff for certain rows or categories of passengers to board first. The impulse for airport-related QJP is so strong that it accompanies me even to my journey's end, when, while deplaning, I jump the implicit queue inside the aircraft all over again by rushing to the front, ahead of those sitting in front of me. I do some queue-jumping even at the random queue in front of the baggage carousel. And once again, as I exit the terminal and encounter a queue for cabs – where, with a wait of five to ten minutes, a cab is more or less assured – I am not beyond trying my I-didn't-notice-you-in-the-queue trick.

In a nutshell, for the queue-jumper in our land, it's a heads-I-win-and-tails-you-lose kind of deal, as there is no disincentive or penalty – formal or social – that visits him at any stage for attempting or executing the jump, even if sometimes you wish the municipal-tap kind of deterrent could be dished out to the queue-jumpers like me then and there. Ah, if only! And of course, this is precisely what emboldens me and my ilk.

Power and Structured Queue-jumping

Often, QJP seems to be derived not so much from one's education or wealth as from one's power; and if the power is state-supported, so much the better. For instance, whether a lowly babu like a tahsildar or a big one like an IAS officer; a modest traffic constable or a mighty IPS officer; a humble party worker or a heady MLA, MP or minister – the worthies who go by the sobriquets of VIPs, VVIPs, VVVIPs et al. in their respective environments, or even the kith and kin of any of these, it comes naturally to them to convert this power into a queue-jumping opportunity, no matter whether the queues are real or virtual, overt or covert, implicit or explicit, at airports, toll booths, sports venues, movie halls or anywhere at all for that matter. Even as these lines were being written, Chandigarh was in the news for demarcating a dedicated lane for 'VVIPs' with red beacons and flags, and another lane for the lesser mortals on public roads.

Of course, as a citizen I resent it intensely. But put me in the same position as those 'VIPs' and rest assured I shall do exactly the same myself. Even in a private wedding, a 'VIP' will be walked right up to the newly wedded couple on the dais, by none less than the parents of the bride or the groom themselves, to greet and bless the young couple. That they are signalling to their other guests lined up in serpentine queues clutching their gifts that they are less important than this 'VIP' bloke never occurs to them, or, if it does, they are not particularly sensitive. As a nation, everyone is supposed to take into account such things and nobody is supposed to take umbrage. As far as I am concerned, if I am suitably empowered per chance, howsoever humbly or grandly, I consider jumping queues to be part of my perquisite.

So ubiquitous is this queue-jumping that now most airports or stadia, for example, have taken to formalizing queue-jumping. They have now provided for separate passages for VIPs to jump queues 'systemically' or 'formally' so that they don't look too bad walking straight to the head of a serpentine queue. Politicians themselves have tried to take their routine queue-jumping to newer levels. As if the élan with which they could sail through our airports ahead of hundreds of travellers was somehow deficient in honour, in 2014 our worthy MPs were appealing to the aviation minister to be allowed to jump over the common man in style, with more privileges at airports, like an escort and a protocol officer, not to mention their security cover, and for their cars to be driven directly to the aircraft! Fortunately, in a rare moment of generosity, they stopped short of asking for a military band to accompany them all the way to the planes.

Of course, not all our airports provide for fast-track passages, which Westerners allow at a premium in their airports to those travelling first class or business class. Nor do they provide for a marhaba-like arrangement (of the Dubai airport), where one pays for the privilege of being ushered through the airport gates faster.

Our system is somewhat different. Our fast-track or marhaba equivalent involves our 'leaders' wearing spotlessly white kurta-pajamas and being escorted by a couple of safari-suited gunmen to the front of any queue. And for this variety of government-sponsored VIPs and their families and friends, we have luxury lounges in our airports with facilities that would leave the best hotels red-faced. It is another matter that more often than not these VIPs with their spouses in tow may be paid for with our tax money. I hate this VIP cult – except when I am a 'VIP' myself.

A neighbour of mine once attempted a rather brazen form of queue-jumping when there was a long line of folks waiting to cast their vote. We had been waiting for some two hours in the queue when this neighbour, the local MLA, all clad in spotless white, came in a swagger, surrounded by scores of hangers-on, and simply walked into the booth to cast his vote, without the leave of those waiting. A bold intervention by those at the head of the line – who told him that this was the hallowed process of democracy at work and that at least here he should stand in line like everybody else – shocked and infuriated him no end. Of course, he predictably asked the challengers if they knew who he was, without realizing it was precisely because he had been recognized that they had chosen to challenge him. But these are of course very rare instances in our democracy – because such open challenging of 'VIP' queue-jumpers can often be seriously injurious to health.

Caste-based Queue-jumping

In some parts of our country, I can jump queues based on caste and creed as well. No one dare challenge me if I am from the higher caste. I have seen districts in Bihar, Uttar Pradesh and Andhra Pradesh (and I am sure there are very many more) where if a pedestrian or a cyclist sees a well-dressed person (who, one can safely assume, is a government servant or someone from a higher socio-economic strata[2]), he gets off the road or dismounts from the bicycle and stands to the side with his head bent until the person has passed. If he is going in the same direction as the said person, he will seriously hesitate to overtake him. The VIPs' place in any queue is simply the foremost, and unchallenged, as those they jump over must watch mutely with bovine resignation.

Learning from Cows

Speaking of bovine resignation, queue-jumping based on our social ranks is evocative of a paper that I came across describing some aspects of the behaviour of cows! The paper on the implications of automated milking on animal welfare observed, 'The cows' interest to go to the waiting area in front of the milking unit depends on the time since last feeding and the number of cows already in the waiting area. Low-ranked cows have to wait longer than the high-ranked ones when queuing and generally choose time periods when the high-ranked are less active!'[3]

Well, one can only say our 'VIPs' have learnt well from the cattle and that cattle share more than our road space with us.

And from Baboons

While no disrespect is implied to anybody, cows and baboons included, it is difficult to overlook the behaviour of baboons in the context of queues. Says a paper on the behaviour of savannah baboons, 'In some periods, the dominance hierarchy [of the baboons] functioned as a queue in which males waited for mating opportunities, so that rank predicted mating success.'[4]

Entitled Queue-jumping

In essence, our social rank and hierarchy are as important to us in determining our queuing etiquette as they are to bovines and simians. Yes, our attitude to queues is as close to nature as it can get.

A heavyweight babu, politician or corporate honcho may walk straight past a long queue in front of a lift and ride to the top of a twenty-two-story building all alone. No one may dare ride alongside him, save his sidekicks.

Nor is that all. These power-wielding, queue-jumping babus, politicos and other bigwigs also have a tacit entitlement to jump virtual queues (VQ1, VQ2 and VQ3) of virtually any kind. The wealthy often do their best to substitute their wealth for power when it comes to jumping queues. I may whine about it but make no mistake; give me half a chance and I shall do exactly the same.

Virtual queues of VQ1 kind, like those for admission in schools and medical or engineering colleges; or for beds in high-end government as well as private hospitals; or for allotment of choicest municipal plots; or for passes for any major event in the city or virtually any product or service that is in short supply – the list is long – are all routinely available for jumping to the VIP queue-jumpers, while non-VIPs find it much more difficult to jump these queues. It is their sheer spirit that keeps them trying to jump such queues. In the north of India, such an attempt is called an 'approach', which goes with a sentence like 'Koi approach hai kya?' meaning, 'Do you know a suitable bigwig who can help jump the queue?' The only ones to complain about such queue-jumping are those who do not have any 'approach'.

Virtual queues of VQ2 type, where people are given a sequential number, are in principle difficult to jump, for the very systemic process of giving out a sequence number is meant to ensure a fair queuing system. Therefore, the power wielders jump these queues not overtly but covertly, for instance, by directly accessing the officials behind the scenes, bypassing the counter altogether. For example, if I am a senior government babu or a politician, I send a junior official directly to the passport or transport officer, and the work happens outside the VQ2 lines meant for lesser mortals. If I am a corporate honcho, I have my 'PR' team to take care of my queue-jumping.

Phone-aided Queue-jumping

Virtual Queues of VQ3 type are easy for the powerful to jump simply because there is no proof of one's place in the queue. However, even for the common folk, phones help to bypass real queues. For example, I know that when I call an enquiry counter or an air ticket booking counter, I typically get priority over the person actually standing in line. But this is not the same as queue-jumping, even if in reality the effect on those already in the queue is similar, namely, a longer wait. While this can be frustrating for the one standing physically in line, it is not easy to escape this form of unwitting queue-jumping unless the service provider decides to set up a separate queue for telephone bookings or enquiries. But try catching me waiting my turn in a queue.

In fact, I came across a website, www.barpass.uo.uk, which advertises its app called B (for Barpass) on its homepage. 'Hate queuing for coffees and drinks?' The site has a solution: 'Don't queue; order and pay for food and drinks through your smart phone and pick them up from a collection point or have them delivered to your table. On top of that, enjoy personalized offers and rewards from your favourite venues.' Of course, this service is not so much queue-jumping as averting queues.

But the matter becomes galling when a telephone booking for a table in a restaurant made with little effort by someone competes with those physically turning up for a table at peak time. So in effect, if I booked the table earlier in the day, I just saunter into the restaurant over the heads of all those standing in line outside. This format of unintended queue-jumping is not explicitly recognized as queue-jumping.

Even so, imagine that you are in a queue for a good twenty minutes outside one of two restaurants of comparable quality of food. One of them gives those with telephonic reservations precedence over you, while the other does not. In which of the two would you feel unfairly treated? It may be that if you were the one making the telephonic reservation, you would prefer the first to the second. But that would be natural because in that case you are a 'queue-jumper' of sorts. But if you are queued up in the second restaurant, you are bound to be peeved at someone jumping over you just because they made a phone call to the restaurant while you were cooling your heels at the entrance.

In the West, precisely owing to such sensitivities, restaurants are increasingly refusing to take telephone bookings for tables. Trust those blokes to find solutions to thwart even the most dignified kind of queue-jumping!

Opportunity Cost of Queues

Considering the alacrity with which I jump queues, it would appear that I must have an enormous opportunity cost of time. So what is my cost?

Let me do a 'back of the envelope' computation. I am an average Indian, so my per capita annual income should be about $1,688 in 2015. That's Rs 113,000 per annum, thanks to the devalued rupee at 67, give or take.

So when I jump a queue and save, say, fifteen minutes of my queuing time, that also saves me a cool Rs 3.7 ($113,000/365/24/4 = 3.7$)! This works out to about Rs 0.25 per minute saved! Now that's serious money.

If you think I am joking, think again. Let us assume that our population under the age of eighteen (about 42 per cent) is not part of the queues of the adults and in any case has zero opportunity cost as they are not yet employed. Thus the opportunity cost is applicable only to 58 per cent of the adult population, or about 725 million people. If these people did not save fifteen minutes each every day of the year by jumping queues, our comptroller and auditor general may peg the loss of GDP at about Rs 1 trillion or Rs 100,000 crore per annum! So we have good justification for jumping queues.

So let us take a cue from the above analysis. Let no one baulk at my queue-jumping trait. Jumping queues is my national pastime. My birthright. And what is more, it pays!

The Physiognomy of an Indian Queue

The Westerners are a wasteful people: big homes, big cars, big energy spend, big personal space – big everything. When they form a queue, they space themselves generously, just as they do while driving, keeping great distance between two vehicles. They take their personal space seriously. They give others their space, both figurative and physical, and expect no less from others. That's why they put those yellow lines a good two metres away from the service counters – so that both the service provider and the receiver have some personal space without the next fellow in line breathing down the neck of the one ahead.

I, a good Indian, on the other hand, am a thrifty fellow. I conserve. Conserve on gift-wrapping papers, on plastic bottles, on polyurethane bags, on cardboard boxes, on notebooks, on sarees – which reappear as curtains or bed covers, then pillowcases and finally as shopping bags. I even recycle the recycled black garbage bags. Not for nothing are my countrymen the world's best conservationists and among the most thrifty people. A large majority of us waste little space on a lavatory. Even the most well-off amongst us rarely 'wastes' a space of more than 7'x7' for the living quarters of our domestic helps. Of two lifts in most buildings, usually we operate only one. Of two gates to a building, we usually keep one locked with chains. Yes, we are a thrifty lot.

That's why I also conserve queuing space, standing behind you in very close proximity, breathing down your neck, brushing your backside with my belly, and that's also why I am not a big respecter of those yellow lines.

My habits, mimicked by millions, contribute to making our queues acquire some distinct characteristics:

Standing Belly by Back: We have all learnt to conserve space in our queues by standing belly by back, as it were.[*] That's why the belly of the guy behind you, often paunchy, must firmly press against the small of your back; or else the queue is neither efficient nor consummated. It doesn't matter if you happen to be at an ATM, needing a bit of privacy; be prepared to feel the hot breath of the guy behind you on your nape. There is enough freedom enshrined in our Constitution for us not to worry unduly about the freedom of personal space. We are given to fill space like water fills up cracks. We are unforgiving of the slightest slack on the part of the one in front of us. Perhaps that's why we stand in queues like a tight pack of cards, lest a queue-jumper insert himself in the gap.

Fuzziness: Our queues have the quality of a beehive, which seems like a solid mass at a distance but a closer look reveals a constant state of flux. So a Martian peering at an Indian queue may see a semblance of a solid queue, but closer home we know that mass is nothing but a horde of elements constantly trying to change their positions.

All in all, queues in India have a fuzzier, more nebulous and more probabilistic character than queues elsewhere in the world, thanks to our arbitrary nature of queue formation, made even fuzzier by queue-jumpers. Because of this fuzziness, in most of our queues, it is difficult to say what the rank order of any one person in the queue is, because the rank is often probabilistic at best.

---

*Comedian Radhika Vaz puts it more colourfully in the *Times of India*, calling it standing 'genitals by bum'.

Three-in-One Queues: The same fuzziness has another manifestation. For example, if our queues are linear at all, they are linear like a plait – often comprising two or even three sub-queues or parallel queues – where no one is quite clear who is actually in the main queue and hence who is ahead of whom. We can have a surreal accumulation of people in a roughly linear formation that is both a queue and yet not-a-queue at the same time, à la light, which is a wave and yet not a wave at the same time.

The best specimen of sub-queues are to be observed immediately after a flight boarding announcement or just as a bus arrives at a stop, or even at supermarket pay booths at peak time, or during weekends when the traffic is heavy. During such times, I and others like me like to beat the main line by making subsidiary queues of our own, each of which becomes a tributary to the larger queue. This happens because as an early queue-jumper, I pretend I did not notice the first queue forming and casually saunter in alongside the first few people in the original queue. Those in the first queue have no strong case to object to me, as I have not directly jumped anyone in that queue (and in the worst-case scenario, where someone from the first main queue does seriously object, why, I deploy the good old tactic of taking a deep breath as if to say how tiresome people can get over the smallest of things, or even pretend to be absent-minded and retreat, with no harm done).

And soon others join behind me, and since all those behind me may be considered as legitimate as those lining up behind the first person in the first queue, my own legitimacy is now safely reinforced.

Now the situation is nearly ripe for the plucking. Before long, the person at the service counter may appeal to everyone to form a single queue. At this juncture, given that there are two or more queues already formed, and no one can really adjudicate who came after whom, the only reasonable thing to do for the service person is to have the different lines merge in some random fashion.

Fortunately, the leadership skill required to form a new queue with our own followers comes easily to us. After all, given the number of queues we come across every single day of our lives, mastering the sense of timing, identifying the right opportunity and ensuring a high degree of success in such queue-jumps are things we start doing early in life.

Believe it or not (Ripley's, please take note), this is what I observed once at one of our airports. There were already three familiar sub-queues at a boarding gate. But if I thought three sub-queues implied that all the people within each sub-queue must follow their line, I was in for a rude surprise. I observed one worthy within a sub-queue making a sub-sub-queue by pretending that he did not notice the person ahead in his sub-queue!

Straddling Two Queues: Standard variants of queue servicing involve two systems: one, where a single queue leads to more than one service counter; and two, when there are as many queues as service counters. One often witnesses the first variant at airports, where a long snake-like queue formed by retractable tapes guides the line to an array of service counters. The second system is what one typically sees at McDonald's.

Such well-defined and unambiguous queuing systems are uncomfortable to a good Indian like me, for they afford fewer opportunities for queue-jumping. A degree of ambiguity in the system is a necessary condition for me to ply my trade. Such ambiguity is usually afforded to a keen pair of eyes like mine when two service centres operating in the second of the above two systems are located very close to each other, like, say, two service counters at a fast food restaurant.

Under these conditions, supposing I am near the head of the queue but not quite, it takes but minimal manipulation to place myself such that nobody behind me quite knows which of the two queues I am really in. As my turn approaches, there is someone ahead of me at each of the two service counters, while I am behind them, straddling both the queues. I smoothly jump to the one that clears first. Of course, this does not get me a large advantage, but for a purist, it is the principle that matters: when you can, jump.

Straddling Two Lines – A Variation: There is a slight variation of the above gambit that I practise every time I can. The cardinal rule of this gambit is simple: if there is more than one independent queue for the same service, and if I have someone, say, my spouse, with me, it is sheer stupidity for both of us to stand in the same line. We must stand in different lines, and depending on who reaches the service window first, the other can simply sidle up alongside. What could be more legitimate? Of course, it is not absolutely essential that this be my spouse. But people are quick to point fingers if I run into a casual acquaintance and leverage this chance encounter to my advantage. The acceptance of this format of queue-jumping is directly proportional to the social legitimacy of the relationship I have with the one accompanying me.

Straddling Two Lanes: Straddling two lanes, akin to straddling two lines, is another of the tricks I routinely practise on our roads. Here is how. Instead of keeping my vehicle to the centre of a lane and following the one ahead of me, I straddle two lanes, keeping the lane divider to the centre of my bonnet so that I can switch between the two, depending on which lane moves faster. What is more, this is not a strategy I use only in traffic jams or otherwise slow-moving traffic. It is equally effective on a freeway. Hogging two lanes keeps the traffic behind me – well, behind me at my mercy.

The Dipper Gambit: This is one strategic bit of knowledge that almost all of us seem to come factory-fitted with.

Let me explain. I once read an account of a one-lane bridge across a creek in Ithaca – the quaint little city-within-a-city in central New York – narrated by the behavioural scientist Richard Thaler.[5] During traffic hours, there are always many cars on either end, waiting to cross the bridge. In a wonderful display of a self-regulated queue, four or five cars will cross the creek and then the next car in that direction will stop to let four or five cars from the other direction to cross, and so on. Now don't get me wrong. I am well aware that this will hardly work in New York proper, leave alone in our cities and towns.

But for the most part in India, when faced with a similar circumstance, we play by very different rules – rules that are purely and exclusively ours. Every Indian knows that if he flashes his high beam repeatedly and urgently, it is equivalent to asserting one's right of way. And mind you, it is not a gentle request for permission to pass first; it is the assertion of a right.

To the best of my knowledge, no law of the land confers this right on any driver. No driving manual mandates this signalling mechanism. No educational institution imparts this nugget of wisdom to its pupils. No other part of the world has a code such as this. But somehow, it has become common practice in our country without one word ever having been said or written about it.

Usually there is a race between the drivers on both sides to be the first to flash their lamps breathlessly. Now that both sides have made an assertion, who should prevail? More often than not, it is the larger vehicle – the plain old 'might is right' rule. If the two vehicles are similarly sized, well, both rush into the aperture head-on, daring the other to chicken out.

What is more, the dipper rule applies even if I am on the wrong side of the road, like when I overtake a vehicle and am on the right (as opposed to the left) side of a single-lane road while you are coming from the opposite direction, keeping to your correct side. So now, we are both on the same side of the narrow road. But if I flash my high beam like the devil possessed, it means I expect you to get off the road and halt so that I can overtake the vehicle in comfort.

Ducking the Railing Tape: I deploy another common gambit in semi-formal queues at airports, amusement parks, etc. When there are only a few people in line and the space between the railings is more or less empty, you may walk zig-zag through half a dozen turns to reach the end of the line while I simply slip under, jump over or unhitch the railings to land ahead of you. I have undoubtedly jumped the line to your front without actually cutting it!

An Aside

We are a touchy lot. Yes, a very touchy lot. If anyone points out to us that there is something very wrong about our queue-jumping or red-light jumping or garbage dumping or open-air defecating or pretty much any other behaviour, we shall be quick to take umbrage – serious umbrage. Not only will we brand the offender unpatriotic, we will also remind him for good measure of our glorious past – in the firm belief that a glorious past is somehow consolation for a sorry present. One is frequently asked, 'Don't the same Indians behave impeccably when they are abroad?' As if behaving correctly abroad is a certification of the fundamental goodness of our souls.

Those who ask that question obviously miss the point that, given our size vis-à-vis that of an average Westerner, if we tried any of our stunts in a foreign land, we would probably invite significant injury. At the same time, we also seem to be blind to the fact that increasingly the reverse is beginning to happen as well. The Westerner who behaves impeccably in his own country feels free to jump queues when on Indian soil! I have seen this umpteen times, including at airports. Perhaps their survival instinct tells them that in this country, that's the only way to get to your destination. Perhaps there is something after all to do in Rome as Romans do.

And probably there is something else at play here – what behavioural scientists call the 'demonstration effect'. Suppose you are waiting to cross a road and the pedestrian signal for you is red. But if enough people around you begin to cross the road anyway, you often have a tendency to join them, right? If so many others are doing it, it must be safe to follow them. To sum up, we often mimic what those around us do.

So maybe when we mimic their behaviour in their land, we are merely mimicking what is demonstrated by them – that is, self-discipline. When they mimic us in our land, they mimic what is demonstrated by us – the inclination for a free-for-all. So no credit to us for behaving well abroad and no discredit to them for behaving badly in our country.

Let me now move on to the psychology of queues, which, sociological differences notwithstanding, exhibits some surprising similarities across the globe.

4

The Psychology of Queues

Entering the local pharmacy, he walked straight up to the head of the queue and announced to the pharmacist, 'Two strips of Digene for my heartburn, please.'

The pharmacist gave him a sharp look and asked, 'What about those already in the line, sir?'

He replied, 'I have no clue about their ailments. They are no kith nor kin of mine.'

Federal Express, the overnight delivery company, once advertised: 'Waiting [to be served] is frustrating, demoralizing, agonizing, aggravating, annoying, time-consuming and incredibly expensive.'[1]

Now who can argue with that? Or that waiting in queues is a waste of time – time flushed down the toilet? And when the queue is particularly long, isn't it natural for us to want to jump it? Unfortunately, when a queue is long, and slow to boot, queue rage may also reach a point where it may not be an altogether unnatural sentiment for those in the line to want to flush the queue-jumper down the toilet as well. Do these frustrations and inconveniences force us to understand the phenomenon of queue-jumping a little more closely?

Have We Researched Queues?

We are a blissful country – blissful because, for the most part, we pretend that problems don't exist, even as they stare us in the face, so that we are not needlessly stressed for lack of solutions. As a consequence, we consider it utterly foolish to spend time and resources searching for ways to inhibit queue-jumping when queue-jumping is not even a recognized problem.

But that does not mean the rest of the world has not viewed queuing and queue-jumping as serious enough matters for research.

While Western scholars have been exercising their brain cells on such questions as how best to speed up queues, how best to reduce the waiting time in queues, how to improve service time – questions that have given birth to the entire field of Queuing Theory – we as a people have been limiting ourselves to honing our queue-jumping skills. But even here, alas, it is the 'jugaad' (make-do approach) that is often put to use; we do not concern ourselves with finding answers to such questions as: What tactics work best for queue-jumpers? Can our queue-jumping skills be improved further through a better understanding of queuers' psychology? How does queuing psychology work? What psychological interventions can make queuing less harrowing and discourage queue rage? What are the best points in a queue at which a queue-jumper can cut in successfully? Who are the people in a queue most likely to object to a queue-jumper? Which are the worst seasons for queue rage? What is the best way to discourage a queue-jumper? What's the cost of not jumping a queue? What is the link between queuing on the one hand and demand and supply on the other? Is queuing linked to the value of the product? What is queue rage? Why does it occur?

We do not seem to realize that finding answers to such questions can certainly make us better queue-jumpers!

But even to find answers to these questions, which are vital to improving our queue-jumping skills, once again we depend on the research of Western scholars belonging to societies which largely abhor queue-jumping. These researches are rich mines of knowledge with which we can arm ourselves to jump queues with greater success, alacrity and élan than ever before.

Queue Rage

Queue rage, as one can surmise, is aggressive or angry behaviour resulting from waiting in line. In theory, queue rage is expected to occur when the service at the counter is too slow or when someone tries to jump the queue, particularly when the queue is long and slow-moving. What is the primary driver of queue rage in our country vis-à-vis the West? With a bit of reflection, we can see that broadly speaking we mostly reserve our impatience for slow-moving services, while Westerners reserve theirs for queue-jumpers.

With us, slow-moving queues can give rise to queue rage directed at service providers and also encourage more queue-jumping. In contrast, Western impatience and outrage is more likely directed at queue-jumpers even as they show infinite patience with slow service.

Take the Germans, who are so disciplined that they do not normally need the highly evolved American 'queue management systems'. But on the rare occasion when someone attempts the jump, things can get ugly very fast. The jump symbolizes a complete breakdown of law and order such that an ordinarily restrained German may not be held accountable if he takes law into his own hands.

Closer home, it is as if we intuitively understand that we cannot be queue-jumpers and also give in to queue rage simultaneously. Just imagine the state of the nation if each one of us, a born queue-jumper, also suffered from queue rage every time someone else jumped a line! Slow service is another matter. But even here, usually some catalyst is required to set the ball rolling. I will stand patiently in a queue for a very long time until someone near the head of the line angrily questions the slow service. And then all hell may break loose as I and many others join in enthusiastically.

The world over, queue rage is often closely connected with road rage. For example, one vehicle jumping a queue can lead to a case of road rage. But then, we are a nation of peaceful citizens and do realize that we simply cannot afford to be riled by this particular fillip to road rage. After all, we do not really believe in queues in the first place, and we believe in the idea of sticking to our lane even less, so that we almost never queue up one behind the other on the roads. We just manoeuvre our way through whatever little gaps we see. So why should we be enraged about someone not following the vehicular queue? Our road rage may be intense because the other guy grazed or dented our vehicle, or because we cannot trust our insurers to pay up, or because we cannot rely on our policemen to take suitable action; but rarely because a guy jumped the lane. As long as the two vehicles escaped meeting in space tangentially, howsoever infinitesimally close they came to a collision, they believe in just going their respective ways. We intuitively understand that in our culture trying to jump a queue is hardly an offence. It is our way of life, which we like to insist we are proud of.

Queue Rage British Style

In Britain, expectedly, queue rage is often for the second reason, namely, when there is an attempt at queue-jumping. I chanced upon this first-hand account of a case of queue rage in the UK on Reddit.

> I was queuing in the ten items or less line in a well-known UK supermarket chain. Just as the cashier was helping one elderly customer bag her items, with the next guy about to unload his items onto the counter, a short woman in a business suit pushed her way in between him and the cashier. I heard her mumble to him, 'Just grabbing lunch, I'm running late,' before chucking her meal deal, which consisted of a sandwich, a bottle of juice and a packet of crisps, onto the counter. I should clarify that I was about

third out of six or seven people in this queue and there was only one ten items or less lane; the store was busy and we were all trying to buy our lunches.

As the cashier was helping the first lady with her bags and credit card, the guy who was supposed to be next in line – without saying a single word to the queue-jumper – picked her bottle of juice off the counter, knelt down and rolled it along the ground towards the back of the queue! She turned to him as he picked up her packet of crisps and chucked it to the back of the queue, too. Her expression will be burned into my memory for eternity. She couldn't legitimately complain, because she, along with everyone around her, was perfectly aware of what she had tried to do. Plus, there was a whole queue of hungry British people observing her now! She stared daggers at the guy she tried to skip, picked up her sandwich, then storming off (a whole five metres) to pick the rest of her lunch off the floor, disappeared back into the aisles in a fit of embarrassed rage. The tension generated in those few moments made me feel proud to be British.[2]

There are more extreme displays of queue rage as well. For example, a news item in the *Daily Mail* referred to a case of queue rage over who was next in line.[3] The newsworthiness of the story was that Cherie Blair, wife of former British prime minister Tony Blair, and a lawyer, had kept the twenty-five-year-old violent offender out of prison because he was a 'religious man'. Another story in the *Daily Mail* reported one Kevin Tripp, fifty-seven, being hit so hard on the head over a rumpus arising from queue-jumping that the man collapsed and died in a pool of blood.[4] And earlier, on 1 February 2004, there was a report in the *Telegraph* about one Daniel Barker, twenty-eight, who had flown into a rage and nearly killed a young man, Adyl Kanata, after being accused of queue-jumping![5] Even being accused of queue-jumping is shameful enough to cause queue rage on that island.

Queuing and Service Experience

Anyone asked to recall their service experience of which waiting in a queue was an integral part will tell us that the duration of the wait significantly affected their overall perception of the quality of service provided. Even when their transaction with a service organization was efficient, courteous and complete, the bitter aftertaste of the time taken to be served, or the shoving and jostling involved to get to the service counter, can make them think of the experience as less than satisfactory.

Queuing Theory has received a great deal of attention from academic researchers, and their results and insights have been successfully applied in a wide variety of settings. However, much of Queuing Theory is concerned with 'queue management' techniques, addressing questions such as: At what rate is the queue forming? At what rate is it being serviced? What is the average waiting time? How can we get 'queue discipline'? What should be the nature of queues? These are all fairly objective questions that elicit fairly provable answers and solutions.

However, questions like which factors have the maximum impact on the overall experience of waiting, which factors can improve the quality of waiting experience, how does the perception of an experience influence the level of satisfaction, how best to reduce complaints and so on have received much less attention. This is unfortunate because poor, long and frustrating waiting experiences are a tinderbox that can explode in queue rage.

We saw in the case of the Houston airport (Chapter 2) experience that waiting itself is an unpleasant proposition. And when one must wait, the quality of the wait becomes key to the customer's overall experience.

Quality of Queuing Experience

That the experience of waiting can make the wait appear long or short should be obvious. For an average individual, waiting in a line in the company of a comely member of the opposite sex can make a half-hour wait seem like no time at all, while waiting on one's own, with nobody to talk to and nothing to do, can make a ten-minute wait feel like an eternity. Waiting in a pleasant air-conditioned environment with something to read can make time fly, while twiddling one's thumbs on the road in conditions of heat, humidity or rain outside the US consulate in Mumbai or Chennai can seem like a never-ending wait.

As Steven Levitt, the well-known American economist of *Freakonomics* fame, remarks, 'Products are consumed, services are experienced.' If so, it may not be enough to focus on minimizing waiting time or such other objective factors alone to measure service experience; it is perhaps equally or even more important to improve subjective factors, like the quality of the waiting experience. Such measures may have the collateral benefit of minimizing queue-jumping, even if an ardent queue-jumper considers it collateral damage as it reduces his or her pleasure arising from queue-jumping.

Psychology of Waiting

Let us see how the psychology of waiting in lines influences one's waiting experience. David Maister of Columbia University offers two general propositions about service encounters and how they are experienced.[6] The first is what he calls 'The First Law of Service', which stated simply is: Satisfaction (S) = Perception (P) – Expectation (E).

For a satisfied client, the perception of service must exceed his expectation. This is intuitively appealing. The perception level remaining the same, if the expectation of service level goes up, the level of satisfaction falls, increasing the element of dissatisfaction, leading to disappointment.

Evidently, both perception and expectation reside in the minds of people and do not represent reality. True, perceptions cannot be altogether dissociated from reality, but they *are not reality*.

Accordingly, if we want people in a queue to have a satisfying experience, we must focus on three things: what we actually did for the client, what the client perceived and what the client expected.

Can all three be managed?

Before I answer that question, let me ask you another

question as a good Indian. Have you ever wondered why in most upmarket hotels there is a mirror just close to the elevators? The answer takes us to the study of Sasser et al.[7]

Sasser's study refers to a well-known hotel group whose guest feedback showed that they were unhappy about the long waiting time for the elevators. The problem was that the guests, while waiting, had nothing to occupy themselves. Little wonder that the bored guests found the wait interminably long.

After some brainstorming on how the waiting experience could be improved, the hotel management hit upon the idea of installing a mirror next to the elevator doors. People with ready access to mirrors are prone to preening, checking their appearances, scrutinizing their paunches in profile and so on, thus keeping themselves busy. While the actual waiting time did not change, the complaints came down significantly. That is to say, the waiting experience was improved by improving people's perception of the wait.

Service providers commonly practise such expectation management. Imagine you are told that you will need to wait in line for five hours outside the US embassy/consulate and you find that actually you had to wait only three hours. Compare this with when you are told the wait will only be an hour and you actually have to wait for three hours. Which three-hour wait appears longer and more frustrating? Many restaurants use this simple technique of managing expectations by giving their guests a waiting time which is much longer than the average waiting time. You are pleased as punch when you end up waiting much less than you anticipated, and your perception of the wait, and hence service quality, goes up significantly!

Such a strategy affects the guest's overall experience. For the waiter, a happier guest is easier to satisfy than a grumpy one. A happier guest is likely to find the food more agreeable than the grumpy one, whose sole objective after the lousy experience of a long wait is to find fault with pretty much everything, not to mention their effect on the size of tips.

This leads us to David Maister's 'Second Law of Service': It's hard to play catch-up ball.

What this means is that if a service is screwed up early on, it is difficult to change the perception with any subsequent attempt at making up. The early stages of a service encounter, of which queues are an integral part, are extremely important in creating the overall perception of service quality. If so, it pays to devote some time, effort and money to ensure that people's early experience of waiting in queues is improved so that their overall satisfaction level goes up. For the same reason, it pays to create systems that would discourage queue-jumpers from spoiling the early experience of those in line.

Perhaps the US of A could easily improve its overall image among developing nations and win more friends by improving the waiting experience in the queues outside their consulates handing out visas – the very early stage of the US of A experience.

Alas! For us, more often than not, the early queuing experience for most services is as repugnant as the subsequent experience of the services themselves, whether the service is renewing a driver's licence, a passport, transferring a gas connection or a car registration. As a result, we are in no danger of experiencing any benefits of such research for a very long time, so that our queue-jumpers may continue with their capers with no imminent threat to their favourite pastime.

But assuming – just assuming – some of our managers – at airports, railways stations or bus stands, if not at government offices – wish to avail of some tools to manage the perceptions and expectations of people queuing up for their services, which in turn could reduce the incentive for queue-jumping, what tools could they use?

Maister presents several propositions relating to the psychology of waiting which I have summed up in the following principles.

Occupied-time Principle

The most difficult thing to do in life is to do absolutely nothing. If you doubt this statement, try closing your eyes, blanking out and guessing the passage of time. If you want a more ready example, think of those two-minute silences we observe from time to time in memory of someone deceased. Aren't they the longest two minutes ever? Probably nine times out of ten, we open our eyes well before the two minutes are past.

The more time you have to do nothing but observe the time pass, the more bored you are, as is evident from the proverb, 'The kettle never boils when you watch it.' Well-known British philologist William Jones once observed,

'Boredom results from being attentive to the passage of time itself.'[8]

There are numerous studies that have researched boredom as a function of passage of time. They all show that those who are more prone to experiencing boredom perceive time as passing very slowly. So when those waiting in a queue have no alternative but to be idle, it compromises their experience of the service.

As a consequence, organizations have come to provide fillers for such periods of time when those in long queues have nothing to do but stand and stare. This has helped pre-empt the boredom that results from the idle time spent in long waiting lines and led to fewer attempts at queue-jumping.

In many cases, this has taken the shape of providing fillers that are related to the services for which the queue may be formed. For example, restaurants often hand out menus to the waiting patrons, so they can peruse the offerings while waiting, with the added benefit that it helps quicken the service once they are seated as the order may already have been placed while still waiting in the queue. This in turn also keeps the restaurant's cash register ringing with a quicker turnover of customers. For the same reason, they also turn their waiting areas into bars – again with obvious benefits to the customers as well as the restaurant. Doctors often provide in their waiting rooms such fillers as health-related posters, weighing scales, height-measuring scales, eye-testing charts, biomass index charts, self-testing blood pressure instruments, charts with the calorific values of various food items and so on. Posters on holiday destinations in travel agencies or on savings products in banks are also examples of fillers.

Fillers may also be deliberately unrelated to the service. For instance, a dentist or a surgeon may put up posters which distract a waiting patient from the painful procedure ahead. But in many cases, the fillers could be random, merely meant to distract the waiting service seeker. For example, some tactics used to keep people occupied include having an exhibition of paintings, a fancy aquarium, an assortment of magazines or coffee-table books, a small bookshop, other little shops or vending machines and so on in the waiting area.

Fillers can take the form of selling something that queuers may purchase casually. For instance, it is not uncommon for fast food joints to have vendors around to sell casual items like bootlaces, flowers or dinky toys to the queuers during lunch hour.

How does one keep a person queued up on the phone more occupied? The sonorous piped music (Muzak) or the repetitive rendering of 'Please wait; you are in queue …' often played by our customer helplines ends up being even more infuriating than the actual wait! Unfortunately, there is nothing much the service providers can do about it but to make more lines available, which is an expensive proposition and can almost never match up to the peak demand.

Logged-in Principle

Not long ago, I was waiting in a long queue at one of the departure gates of Newark Liberty International Airport in New Jersey. The boarding had been announced, but, for some reason, the actual process had not started and the line was getting fidgety. Suddenly, the staff at the boarding gate started calling out groups of five or six names at random. As the passengers concerned went up to the gate, the airline official took down (or pretended to take down) some detail before proceeding to call the next batch of passengers. In this way the official ended up calling nearly 50 to 60 per cent of the waiting passengers, who walked up to the counter and then went back to their positions in the line. As a frequent flyer of several decades, I did not recall ever witnessing any such 'roll call', which in any case did not cover 100 per cent of the passengers (I wasn't called, for example). Soon it became clear that the only purpose this strange exercise was serving was to make it appear as if the boarding process had commenced, which in turn resulted in the restiveness of the passengers going down significantly! It is the same purpose that handing out menus serves. It creates the perception that the service has already commenced even as you are waiting! 'You are logged in' as it were.

The perception of service experience depends a great deal on whether or not a human contact has been made with the one waiting in line. Human contact reassures the waiting individuals that their presence has been taken due note of and that they will be served. This results in the perception that the service has already commenced. The earlier the human contact in the service chain, the higher the level of satisfaction. According to Maister, pre-process waits are perceived as longer than in-process waits.

This is perhaps also the reason why waiting for five minutes on the phone to be served by the call centre employee is far more annoying than waiting for the same duration in a real queue. In real queues, even when you are not served by a human while waiting, you still see a human performing the service function at the head of the queue, and you can also see other human beings suffering the same experience as you. This is not the case with phone lines. With no human contact, you don't know if you have been 'forgotten'.

People like to get started sooner rather than later. So engage them early with a human interface. And if such measures help curb queue-jumping, so much the better.

Anxiety Principle

Besides the feeling of being 'forgotten' on the phone line, 'the other line always moves faster' and 'should I or shouldn't I change my line' are other queue-related anxieties.

How can such anxiety be assuaged? A reassuring message to those waiting in line often helps. Imagine being caught, after a delayed flight, in a long queue for the boarding pass for a connecting flight, with departure due in forty-five minutes. Every single minute seems interminably long. How you wish you could ask those ahead of you to let you jump the queue. Now imagine an airline staffer telling you not to worry because the flight will be kept on hold to accommodate the passengers from the delayed flight. Your anxiety drops immediately and the wait no longer seems so long. The deep-seated desire to jump the queue is kept in check.

In other words, anxiety can make waiting seem longer than it is.

Uncertain Waits Seem Longer than Known, Finite Waits

Imagine you are joining a long queue to renew your driver's licence just before 9 a.m. at the regional transport office. The service window is supposed to open at 9 a.m. It is already 9.10 a.m. and there is no sign of the window opening. Supposing you are told that the window will now open only at 10. You are frustrated initially but then settle down for the inevitable wait. On the other hand, had there been no information at all about how long you would have to wait, or, worse still, you were told the clerk at the window would appear soon but he actually turns up only at 10 a.m., the wait is bound to feel much longer and way more frustrating even though in reality both the waits were of equal duration.

If you arrive fifteen minutes early for a meeting, you wait patiently until the appointed time. Knowing certainly that the meeting is not scheduled for another fifteen minutes makes the wait tolerable, if not altogether a pleasure. But once the appointed time has passed and you have no information about when the person you are there to meet will show up, you enter a period of uncertainty and the next fifteen minutes appear to drag on.

I had the following experience as I was re-working this

chapter. A highly educated and brilliant thirty-year-old entrepreneur, the son of a longstanding friend, called me one day from the Delhi international airport and told me that it had taken him two hours to clear the check-in procedure and reach the security line. I promptly shared the feedback with the airport CEO, who I knew would do his best to improve the airport's performance. The next day, the CEO informed me on the basis of CCTV time stamps that it had taken the entrepreneur eighty-two minutes (conceding that this too was a long wait) to get through the entire process because of some glitches that day. Clearly when the wait was uncertain and perceived to be devoid of any value whatsoever, the waiting time seemed inordinately long.

Time perceptions can get seriously distorted, and none of us is spared of such distortion!

Elucidation Principle

When you queue up for public transport during heavy rains or rush hour, you are prepared to wait longer than you would when the weather is fine and it is not peak time. When you are seated inside an aircraft and it is past the take-off time, with no announcement explaining the delay, the wait becomes oppressive. But when an announcement explains that the wait is on account of two passengers on a connecting flight which was delayed by fifteen minutes, the wait is no longer as oppressive.

The explanation is more about feeling respected and empowered than knowing the actual waiting time. The explanations also have to be justifiable or reasonable if they are to soothe frayed nerves. The hollow-sounding reason often given for the delay of a flight – late arrival of the incoming aircraft – hardly sounds like a reasonable explanation to soothe tattered nerves.

I remember once waiting in line to have my car serviced. It was a long wait and at least two of the mechanics were just sitting around smoking in public view, making me and some of the others in the line seethe with irritation. I approached the manager of the service centre for an explanation, and he mentioned that the two young mechanics had worked six hours straight and were just taking a fifteen-minute break. None of us was irritable anymore and the quality of the wait improved immediately. For similar reasons, many fast food chains instruct their personnel to take breaks out of the sight of waiting customers.

Fairness Principle

We often find ourselves in queues which are irrationally organized so that the FCFS principle is violated. Those who came after us get ahead even though nobody has jumped the queue. This can happen when a new service window is suddenly opened and those at the tail end of the queue are allowed to rush to this new window and served ahead of those who were in fact way ahead in the original queue. Such an unfair wait is most annoying. It is the same when we are entitled to a faster queue but are put in a slower one. For example, if you have a business class ticket but there is no fast-track access, you are forced to use the regular queue, and you find the experience dissatisfying.

Not all violations of FCFS lead to dissatisfaction, though. For example, when you are waiting at a clinic and a seriously ill patient arrives; or when you are waiting at a restaurant in a group of four and the maitre d' takes the couple that arrived after you because a table for two just became available. These instances, even if they add to one's waiting time, are often perceived as equitable and hence do not vitiate the waiting experience.

A service provider, if he wishes to give his patrons a satisfying experience, must give due regard to FCFS. What the patrons regard as equitable may or may not always be obvious but the perception needs to be carefully managed nevertheless. Often the fairness principle goes hand-in-hand with the elucidation principle. When in doubt, explain.

The Value Principle

We are always willing to wait in a long line to dine at a fancy restaurant but not at the wayside eatery. When we have a full cart of groceries in a supermarket, we are more inclined to accept a long wait in the line than we are when we just want to pick up a loaf of bread and a bottle of coke. This is because we expect some proportionality between the length of the wait and the value we place on our transaction. That is why multiplexes often have a separate line to issue tickets to those who have purchased them online and paid a convenience fee. It is for the same reason that supermarkets often provide an express checkout for those with five items or less, and also why airlines provide for a separate line for passengers without check-in baggage.

When waiting for a doctor, we stay patient for a longer duration if the doctor is a celebrity than we would if he is a cub house surgeon. We are willing to wait for a doctor more willingly much longer if our ailment is serious, as compared to when we are visiting a doctor for the seasonal flu. We are more patient while waiting in a queue to check into a hotel than when we are in line to check out; or while waiting to get into a restaurant versus waiting for the bill to be settled. Why? Because the wait now has a much diminished value.

Group Principle

We discussed earlier how quickly the waiting time in a line passes when we are in pleasant company, as compared to when we are on our own. This is equally true for any company that you may have. A wait in a group always seems shorter than a wait on one's own. This may be on account of several reasons. First, when you are in a group, you are distracted; you have company to share your frustration with; you have the satisfaction that you are all in the same boat. The group develops a camaraderie of its own and it improves the waiting experience.

It is a common observation that people often stand for long in lines without any interaction with each other. Time seems to pass slowly at such times. But as soon as an announcement is made regarding a delay or a change in a flight's boarding gate, there is sudden chatter among those in the line. They share their frustrations with each other and crack a good joke or curse the service provider. Suddenly time jerks forward a tad faster.

The Apology Principle

One can think of other parameters that impact the quality of waiting time in real or virtual queues. In long and delayed lines, an announced and explicit apology or compensation can go a long way in improving the waiting experience. For example, an airline providing free lunch for a delayed flight can significantly improve the quality of the waiting experience.

A sensitive service provider can improve customer satisfaction considerably by improving the waiting experience. Queuing psychology seems to have been mastered by most theme parks across the world. According to the creative vice-president of interactives at Walt Disney Imagineering, which develops Disney parks and resorts, they 'like to view [queues] as the first scene in the story, whatever the story of that particular attraction is'.[9]

Expectations from Indian Service Providers

To an onlooker on average, Indian queuers may appear not to be among the best behaved in the world. But then nor do our service providers provide their queuers comparable distraction, entertainment or value proposition as their counterparts elsewhere. Most queues in our government systems, such as for driver's licences; for passports; for land registration; in land record offices; in rail or road stations; in property tax offices; in ration shops; in gas agencies; at electricity boards and so forth are all completely devoid of any pleasantness of waiting experience. Nor may we reasonably hope for any in the foreseeable future. Expecting these 'service' providers to appreciate the research in the psychology of waiting in lines is like – to translate a Hindi idiom – playing a flute before a buffalo (in expectation of its appreciation).

As a consequence, in most government-led service systems, the only way to minimize one's unpleasant waiting experience seems to be to minimize one's waiting time, even if that has to be achieved through queue-jumping. However, we do have hopes from our service organizations in the private sector, especially those in hospitality, travel and transport services. They can benefit from these ideas in improving the waiting experience of their patrons. But more importantly, if a better waiting experience can have the effect of bringing down some of the queue-jumping, that effect alone will add manifold to the quality of the waiting experience.

No less important is it for these organizations to have a clearly stated queue-jumping policy. Such a policy delineates under what circumstances the person at the counter is empowered to permit a customer to jump an FCFS queue. Under what circumstances can a waitlist order be changed? Which medical cases may be considered more serious? What rights can a paramedic have to decide which medical case is more of an emergency?

Other Behavioural Researches on Queuers

Researchers have also investigated the impatience of customers as exemplified in people simply quitting the queue after a while. It is not unusual for us to abandon the call while waiting for an agent to respond on the phone, or to walk out of a store while waiting for a shopkeeper to attend to us, or to close the page while waiting for a slow internet transaction to be completed. Such studies have tried to investigate how patience and service time may be unrelated, how impatience varies across different customers, how people respond to announcements, etc.

But these studies are of little value to the keen queue-jumper focused on honing his skills, and hence I avoid going into any further details, moving on instead to the next chapter for some useful lessons for my key stakeholders, namely, queue-jumpers.

5

Useful Lessons in Effective Queue-jumping

A woman was leaving a cafe with her morning coffee when she noticed a most unusual funeral procession. A coffin was followed by a second one about 50 feet behind. Behind the second coffin was a solitary woman walking with a black dog. Behind her was a queue of 200 women walking in single file. The woman couldn't overcome her curiosity.

She approached the woman walking with the dog. 'I am so sorry for your loss, and I know now is a bad time to disturb you, but I've never seen a funeral like this with so many of you walking in a single line. Whose funeral is it?' she asked.

The woman replied, 'Well, that first coffin is for my husband.'

'What happened to him?'

The woman replied, 'My dog attacked and killed him.'

She enquired further, 'Well, who is in the second coffin?'

The woman answered, 'My mother-in-law. She was trying to help her son when the dog attacked and killed her also.'

A thoughtful moment of silence passed between the two women. Then the first one asked in excitement, 'Can I borrow the dog?'

The woman replied, 'Join the queue.'

To say that successful queue-jumping can be a very rewarding experience, especially if one is not terribly fussy about scruples and fairness, is stating the obvious. The reverse, namely, having someone else jump over us, can be way more annoying. Fortunately, fairness and scruples are largely irrelevant in a country where very little is fair in any case – or, put differently, almost anything is fair. With nearly everybody resorting to queue-jumping nonchalantly, why shouldn't I? After all, everybody is doing it. How can I alone change the world around me? Ah, the twin defences of a fatalistic nation!

Burdened with such fatalism, one not only jumps queues with gay abandon but in a rare display of empathy for another's point of view also shows considerable tolerance when others jump queues. After all, in our society there is little social stigma attached to queue-jumping, unlike in the West.

But if one is in the small minority of scrupulous queuers, the experience is indeed most frustrating. It is not just the loss of time and place in the queue that is offensive but also the violation of a basic sense of fairness. Added to that is the uncaring attitude of a large majority in the wake of such a flagrant act. It is tragic, almost, that neither the social nor the legal system baulks at such queue-jumping. It is insulting that as a people we should care so little for the feelings of others. It mocks democracy when egalitarianism is so blatantly given short shrift by the state itself in the form of VIP culture. The inadequacy of a society in which fairness finds place neither in the warp nor the weft of the social fabric rankles. The worst of the tragedy is that queue-jumping poses no danger to our social fabric because it *is* the social fabric, complete with faster queues for the 'VIPs' everywhere, including in the legal system.

Research Is Not for Us

This brings us to a logical question, namely: if queue-jumping, with or without social sanction, is offensive to me when I am at the receiving end, surely it must be equally offensive to everybody when they are at the receiving end? If so, why don't scrupulous queuers object more vociferously to queue-jumpers? How often, and which category of people in a queue, object to queue-jumpers? After all, all queue-jumpers must have serious stake in the answers to such simple questions if they are to improve their craft. And helping improve their craft is what this book is about anyway.

But let's face it. With due apologies, yet another of our traits as a people is that we are incapable of providing simple answers to straight questions. More often than not, for every question asked, we receive a barrage of counter-questions in return. Trying to reduce an issue to its basic elements and figuring them out is simply not for us. Providing a simple answer to a question is too much effort because it calls for an organized mind and methodology while we are really a nation of jugaad. We live our lives trying to find a solution to each problem individually rather than find research-based systemic answers for an entire category of problems. In our way of life, research is tedious business with little pay-off and with nothing but expenses to show in terms of time, money and efforts. We abhor tedium; and hence we abhor research. That's why no one accuses us of being a research-driven nation. Thus blame-free, we are a happy lot.

Milgram's Research

But the above questions apparently bothered the trio of Milgram, Toledo and Wackenhut sufficiently for them to try and answer them in 1988.[1] If you have plans to jump queues in the West, you would do well to learn the outcomes of the researches of these gentlemen.

The three studied 129 queues in places ranging from railway stations to betting shops and elsewhere all around New York to investigate how often, and who in a queue, objected to queue-jumpers. They engaged volunteers to jump queues, following a standard protocol in all cases:

1. They always entered the queue between the third and fourth people.
2. The words, said in a neutral tone, were standardized: 'Excuse me, I'd like to get in here.'
3. They stepped into the queue and faced forward.

4. They left the queue when someone challenged their action or reproved them for it or after one minute, whichever was earlier.

The three found that mostly the responses of those in the queue were rather meek. Only in about 10 per cent of the cases were the queue-jumpers literally ejected from the line. Also, only in about 50 per cent of the cases did anyone do anything at all. This included dirty looks as well as verbal and non-verbal objections.

Milgram et al. proceeded to try out two variations to explore the conditions in which people objected to the queue-jumping. Their first variation was in terms of the number of intruders.

When a single person jumped a line, about 54 per cent of the time someone or the other in the queue objected. The success rate of such a jumper was nearly 46 per cent. However, when two people intruded at the same time, the percentage of objections jumped to 91.3.

The second variation involved a 'buffer' person or persons to explore the position of those challenging the queue-jumper. The experimenters asked some volunteers to join the queue legitimately and told them to do nothing but wait patiently in line. When the queue-jumper jumped the line directly in front of the passive experimenter introduced into the line, and the passive experimenter, as directed, did not object, there were objections from others only 25 per cent of the time. When the intruder was introduced in front of two successively placed passive experimenters, the objections dropped to 5 per cent.

It was evident that what the passive bystanders

immediately behind the intruder did or did not do had a direct effect on the behaviour of the others. This implied that while in general one could jump queues with a 46 per cent chance of success with just some grunts and raised eyebrows, the success rate rose to nearly 75 per cent if the person you were jumping ahead of did not mind the intrusion, and rose to virtually 95 per cent if the second fellow behind the one you jumped ahead of also chose not to object.

The results seem to suggest that queue-jumping is tolerated as long as it does not threaten the queue too much. As long as very few people as compared to the total number of people in the queue are trying to cut in, the queue-jumping is tolerated. But if a large number of people try and jump the queue, its very existence is endangered. This tolerance of queue-jumping by the few is surprising but convincing (and of immense utility for our home-grown queue-jumpers as we shall see presently). This behaviour is what we all usually observe. I am sure most of us have experienced it innumerable times, most often perhaps in the queues at X-ray machines in airports. You may be at the head of the line, removing your laptop from the briefcase, and in the split second between your placing your briefcase and then the laptop tray on the conveyor belt, a queue-jumper standing just behind you tries to cut in with his bag. And if you happen to protest, chances are nothing comes of it. One would expect everyone in the queue behind you to object to the queue-jumper; but they don't.

Why Don't Most People Object?

There may be several reasons for this:

1. Those close to the point of intrusion are the likeliest to notice the intrusion. Conversely, those farther behind are less likely to notice it.

2. Those in the line may not have observed that this was a case of queue-jumping, or may have been under the impression that two people were squabbling over their relative positions in the queue; or that the queue-jumper was moving in as part of the acceptable practice of 'place-keeping' and so on. With uncertain information about the specifics of the case, they are more likely to be hesitant to object.

3. A prolonged challenge to the queue-jumper could jeopardize one's own place in the queue as others ignore both the squabblers and simply press on.

4. Social norms regard those directly behind the point of intrusion to be responsible to defend that spot. If everyone defended the spot just in front of them, queue-jumpers would soon be effectively discouraged. Thus, one is expected to object to queue-jumping at least directly in front of them. Also, if social systems do not tolerate some measure of deviance from expected behaviour, they are bound to break down quickly into ungainly fights, delaying everybody else. Occasional queue-jumping (with good reasons maybe) is par for the course, it appears.

5. A queue-jumper robs everyone behind him of the same amount of time, say, five minutes. But those farther back in the line are delayed by only a small fraction of their total waiting time in the queue, while the one immediately behind the intruder may have to wait

twice as long. Hence, it is only reasonable that the onus of defending his place in the queue falls on the one just behind the queue-jumper.

6. The queue also probably tacitly co-opts those who threaten it in the hope that it would ensure that the interests of the aggressors would be aligned with that of the queue and hence the queue would become stronger. Personally I find this argument a little farfetched. Going by this logic, Indian queues must be among the strongest in the world for the sheer numbers of queue-jumpers they usually accommodate. But that is hardly the case.

7. And lastly people are so disgusted with a queue-jumper and view him with such contempt that they do not think it worth their while to make a big fuss. While this may well be true elsewhere, for us, with no social stigma attached to queue-jumping in our country, this reason seems less likely to be applicable.

Based on the above findings, queue-jumpers could have several useful takeaways.

Some Key Lessons

Don't jump the queue in front of a muscleman

Even in highly QJP-resistant societies, it is essentially the person you displace in the queue who matters most in determining the success or failure of your queue-jumping effort. You don't need to be concerned as much about the rest of the queue. If experience is any guide, this happily applies in our land as well. It is a healthy practice to avoid jumping a queue directly in front of a fellow with six packs who towers six inches above you. If you must jump the line, do it in front of a gentle old lady or someone equally innocuous. The research by Milgram et al. tells us that when you are challenged, if at all, it will most likely be by the person you are jumping directly in front of. By carefully selecting the person to jump ahead of, we improve our odds to nearly three-fourths!

Keep an eye on the bloke just behind the one in front of whom you are cutting in

Before executing your queue-jump, it will pay off to pay attention to the fellow directly behind the person in front of whom you cut in. This is because if neither of the first two blokes objects to your jumping, the probability that you will get away with your ploy rises to 95 per cent!

A Pertinent Question

What if the queue has no granny but all musclemen? In such a situation, any attempt at jumping the queue at any point could be injurious to health. But if you are a dedicated queue-jumper, what should you do? How can you improve your odds? Luckily, as far back as 1978, Ellen Langer, a Harvard social psychologist, picked up for deeper investigation this simple question, namely, 'What's the best way to persuade someone to let you jump the queue?'[2]

To answer this question, she conducted an experiment in which her team of researchers worked on queues at photocopiers. The study provided some interesting insights. It was evident that few were willing to suffer those who simply tried to muscle their way through. It was a disastrous strategy. Asking the individual at the head of the queue for permission to cut in was typically much more effective. It was found that nearly 60 per cent of people in the queue acquiesced to such a request, even if the request was as inane as: 'Excuse me, I have a few pages to photocopy. May I use the machine?' However, the request became vastly more effective – nearly 94 per cent relented – if the queue-jumpers added a reason as to why they needed to jump to the front of the queue. Remarkably, a simple reason like, 'Excuse me, I have a few pages for photocopying. May I use the machine because I am in a hurry?' served the purpose fine.

Langer then proceeded to investigate which reasons were the most effective. To her astonishment, she found that it really did not matter what reason one proffered for jumping the queue. For instance, you could shrink your request down to a reason as simple as, 'Excuse me, may I go first because I only have a few copies to make?' Its success rate was found to be 93 per cent! In the end, all that mattered was that you gave a reason – any reason. It was almost as if people simply stopped listening after 'because' and yielded simply to the queue-jumper's having adduced a reason. Langer was able to verify her findings in several of her studies.

Her findings are also what Robert Cialdini refers to in his opening chapter of the path-breaking *Influence: The Psychology of Persuasion* as an automatic response to a certain stimulus.[3]

It seems like most airlines have taken their cue from Langer's work. Why else would they believe providing an inane reason for a delayed departure, such as, 'The delay in departure is owing to the late arrival of the aircraft,' works to assuage the waiting passengers' ire? This reminds me of my little niece. When she was three, she had once asked me, as we had stood next to a lift, 'Why does the lift go up?' As I struggled to respond, she piped up. 'I know! Because it is not going down!'

Are Langer's findings still relevant, nearly four decades later? Or could it be that in the fast-moving world of today, people are far more impatient and hardly disposed to such generosity? The answer, you guessed it, is, 'The findings are still relevant.' Human nature does not change in four decades.

Always give a reason – howsoever absurd – when you jump a queue

It is clear as daylight. If you are going to jump a queue, you might as well use a strategy which is more gracious and more effective in convincing others to agree to your request. You can make it both, by providing a strong reason to jump the queue – never mind even if it looks obvious, lame or even downright silly.

But beware! Though rare, there is always the small possibility of physical retribution for queue-jumping if you blatantly disregard the usually gentle social pressure. *The Malaysian Insider* reported in 2013 that an eighteen-year-old guy was bludgeoned to death in Malaysia after he tried to jump a queue at a food counter.[4] No point rushing to join a queue only to end up meeting your maker, howsoever small the probability.

Financial inducement

Since we are looking at ways to jump queues, we might as well leave nothing to chance. If so, it is bound to cross your mind whether you could improve your odds with a financial inducement to someone in the line to permit you to take his place for a price.

Again, asking a simple question like this to an average intelligent Indian is bound to get you rather involved answers like: It depends on what queue one is standing in; how important it is; what one is planning to do shortly afterwards; the amount of money being offered; one's wealth level; one's mood just then; whether the inducement is in cash, cheque, gift hampers or in promissory notes; one's utility function for time and money, and what have you. But the essence of the simple question would remain unanswered.

Fortunately, Felix Olberholzer-Gee, a Harvard economist, has studied the effect of offering a financial inducement in lieu of a reason to coax people to allow queue-jumping.[5] He had his researchers approach people in queues at random and offer them cash to cut in. Expectedly, the likelihood of being able to jump the queue increased with the size of the cash inducement offered. Also, rarely did anyone down the line object to the financial inducement being offered to someone up ahead in the line. But what was really surprising was that hardly anyone who agreed to let someone jump the queue actually accepted the money offered. And those most likely to accept the cash were students and women. Evidence showed that people treated the amount of money offered as a proxy for the acuteness of the queue-jumper's need to cut in and were largely agreeable to let him in the queue without actually accepting the cash! This goes on to show that Langer was still relevant and right. It was essentially the act of providing a reason that did the trick, with money acting as a proxy for the reason. You may want to wager your money a few times to learn if this would work in our own country or with our countrymen.

Incidentally, paying to jump a queue is not all that farfetched an idea. The fast-tracking of queues is just a more systematic and formalized version of this phenomenon.

When retreat is the best strategy

Every now and then you may encounter a smart alec who will give you a taste of your own medicine. Suppose you are in the photocopier queue and say something like, 'Excuse me, may I go first because I have only a few copies to make?' The fellow you are saying this to may come back politely and firmly, telling you that he isn't in the line to launder his clothes. In such a case, the best strategy undoubtedly is to tuck one's tail between one's legs and beat a quiet and hasty retreat to the end of the queue.

A word of caution to the queue-enraged

Do avoid murder at all cost. In a country where everyone jumps queues unabashedly, such a tendency may also well lead to mass murder.

We may have gained some useful tips about how to be more effective queue-jumpers, but we still need to understand what makes us jump queues at one time or the other and why those in the line allow queue-jumpers to cut in on some occasions but not on others. Let us find some answers in the next chapter.

6

Game Theory and Queue-jumpers

'Nobody gives way to anybody. Everyone just angles, points, dives directly towards his destination, pretending it is an all-or-nothing gamble. People glare at one another and fight for manoeuvring space. All parties are equally determined to get the right-of-way – insist on it. They swerve away at the last possible moment, giving scant inches to spare. The victor goes forward, no time for a victory grin, already engaging in another contest of will. Saigon traffic is Vietnamese life, a continuous charade of posturing, bluffing, fast moves, tenacity and surrenders.'[1]

Gad Allon, an associate professor of managerial economics and decision sciences at the Kellogg School of Management in the US, and Eran Hanany, a professor at Israel's Tel Aviv University, give us the happy assurance that 'there are systems in which cutting in line – and letting others cut in – is a social norm that can actually be beneficial to the system and its customers in the long run'.[2] So, as a people, we may well draw solace from the fact that we are practitioners of such a 'socially beneficial system'. We can legitimately regard ourselves as being rather scientific, even if unwittingly, adding value to the social system through our relentless queue-jumping.

How Queue-jumping Can Be Socially Beneficial

Standing or wanting to join a social queue involves decisions. The queue-jumpers must decide if and when to make the attempt; while those in a queue must decide whether or not to permit someone to cut the line. Formal literature on queue-jumping describes what customers experience as 'tension between social norms and economic reasoning, the latter acting as a force that pushes customers to violate the norms'.[3]

For the time being, we shall ignore the Indian peculiarity, where it is not so much decision-making as reflex. Also, for us, since society is fairly permissive about queue-jumping, there is little 'tension' of the sort described in the sentence above. That leaves only our self-interest to be reckoned with, and our decision is nearly always clear: it is worth our while to jump the queue.

The Indian exception notwithstanding, Allon and Hanany inform us that traditional literature on queue-jumping disregards two important considerations. One, that normative and selective queue-jumping may be value-enhancing for the customers as well as the service managers in the long run, and two, following the socially accepted norms of queue-jumping (such as allowing a wife to join her husband in the queue ahead of others, or taking a five-minute break from the queue without losing one's position in it, etc.) may be consistent with economic value maximization. And it turns out that Evan Schwartz, well-known American author who writes on innovation, pointed this out nearly four decades ago when he held that it is not as if orderly social queues are necessarily devoted to FCFS but may merely be a way of achieving an equilibrium between the more and the less impatient customers (the former being the queue-jumpers).[4]

In Chapter 5 I dealt with Milgram's researches which show that giving a reason for queue-jumping – any reason at all – is usually an effective strategy for jumping queues. We are all used to queue-jumpers mumbling: 'Oh, I am about to miss my flight/train,' or 'Oh, I just have a short question to ask,' and so on, when ideally an inane statement like, 'I need to cut in because I have to get across quickly…' will do just as well.

Whatever the excuse extended, we let folks cut lines sometimes. And we resist them at other times. There is very little literature that explains exactly what stimulates some worthies to try cutting a line and those in the line to allow the queue-jumpers to cut in sometimes but to prevent them at other times. The duo of Allon and Hanany has tried to answer precisely these questions.

Do Unto Others as You Would Have Them Do Unto You

According to the researchers, when someone in a queue permits a queue-jumper in, he is essentially trying to live by the golden rule, namely, 'Do unto others as you would have them do unto you.' The one who permits line-cutting probably thinks, 'My need at the moment is not all that urgent; but I may have an urgent need in the future, when I hope you or someone else like you will let me cut the queue,' and so he gives way in the rational expectation that society will reciprocate his gesture in his time of need.

The Allon-Hanany model is predicated on three key assumptions:

a) That one has a legitimate reason for jumping the line;
b) that everyone at one time or the other will need to jump a queue for similar reasons; and
c) that it is often difficult for those in the queue to verify the queue-jumper's claim (like when he says he only has a brief question to ask the service provider) when the claim is made, but it can be verified later (like whether or not he actually confined himself to a brief question).

They set up a series of game-theoretic situations in which customers with different levels of urgency wait for a variety of services.

Game theory, according to Encyclopedia Britannica, is a 'branch of applied mathematics that provides tools for analyzing situations in which parties, called players, make decisions that are interdependent. This interdependence causes each player to consider the other player's possible decisions, or strategies, in formulating his own strategy. A solution to a game describes the optimal decisions of the players, who may have similar, opposed, or mixed interests, and the outcomes [called equilibria] that may result from these decisions.'

For example, Allon and Hanany describe a series of game-theoretic situations in which, at a doctor's clinic, the services range from giving prescription renewals to attending to medical emergencies. The clinic does not control the queue but informally empowers those in it to regulate themselves as they see best. Thus, a patient can choose whether or not to cut a queue. Similarly, those already in the queue may decide whether or not to allow a queue-jumper to jump ahead.

In order to characterize the different equilibria that could possibly result under different situations, the researchers subject their test customers to both a one-time as well as iterative versions of different situations.

In a one-time or single-stage version of the game, the customers arrive to be serviced and decide whether to join the end of the queue or jump the line. At the same time, each customer confronted with a queue-jumper decides whether or not to allow him to jump. They find that when customers have to play the game only once, they are predominantly guided by the FCFS rule. That is, in a single-stage game, queue-jumping is severely discouraged.

In this version, when a customer jumps the queue, all others in the queue become aware of the intrusion. This basic model then becomes a benchmark for studying more complex systems with special features. For example, in an advanced version, customers decide whether or not to jump queues based on their positions in them. In some other versions, only a small fraction of the entire customer base is present at any point in time. They are permitted private signals to indicate the intrusion so that the customer immediately behind the intruder receives a signal while others do not. In some situations, even when a customer observes an intruder, he cannot spread the information to others immediately as only a small fraction of the customers are present and there is no ready punishment system for the deviants. This calls for a sophisticated punishment strategy which can inform other customers about the presence of deviants in the system who ought to be punished.

But in an iterative game – that is, when the situation repeats itself (going to the clinic again and again) – becomes more complex. In this version, the customers make up their minds whether or not to jump the queue before observing the state of the queue each time, and so on.

A Socially Desirable Equilibrium

The final result seems to suggest that when players engage in iterative versions of the games, the FCFS principle no longer dominates the situation. The pattern changes. It is not unusual for those in the line to let someone with a more urgent need or one who needs a very short consultation to jump the queue. Interestingly, this is true even when those in the line cannot be certain that the would-be queue-jumper's stated reason is legitimate or true.

The results also show that if the customers are patient enough, legitimate intrusions may be used to improve the systemic performance, so that legitimate queue-jumping becomes part of the norm.

The findings also explain why in queues for one-time events or rationed products, queue-jumping is severely discouraged. Try jumping the ticket queue for an India-Pakistan cricket match at a stadium, for instance. These queues tend to be like a one-time game, in a game theoretic sense. On the other hand, social queues at airports, train stations or bus stops mimic iterative games, situations which people face over and over again. And this is where giving each other permission to jump queues for a legitimate reason becomes part of the social norm.

Allon and Hanany conclude that their findings have practical utility. They suggest that service providers should integrate the social norms involved in queue-jumping into their queuing designs. They believe that appropriate signage could help provide suitable pointers to the queuers. For example, a signage at the check-in area of an airport could say, 'Please allow those whose flight departs in less than forty minutes to move ahead.' They also suggest that in some cases the ropes demarcating the lines should be avoided so as to facilitate legitimate queue-jumping.

More specifically, they recommend models that could be useful for a system manager to decide if and when a managerial intervention is required to improve the queue's performance, which is part of the customer's overall service experience, and when it may be best to simply depend on the wisdom of the crowds to take care of themselves.

So, according to Allon and Hanany, flexible queuing systems may improve customer service.

So Have We Got It Right After All?

Well, leaving it to the wisdom of the crowds is what we in this country do best in any case! Could it be that, with our ancient wisdom, we have been doing things right all along? Could it be that we have long since integrated queue-jumping into our social norms, our ethos, our culture, nay, our very DNA?

Only the naïve will believe that Allon and Hanany have the 'I, me and myself' kind of Indians in mind in their researches. We know well as a people that we are expert exploiters of loopholes in systems. Put up a signage asking people to 'make way for those whose flight is about to depart soon', as suggested by Allon and Hanany, and we will find every Indian traveller turning up at the airport at the last moment, demanding to be allowed to jump the queue rather than respect the placard as an appeal meant for exceptional situations. Or, remove the queue fencing and the Indian queue-jumpers will form a dozen different 'queues' when there are only two service counters.

Let us consider the legitimacy of a request for queue-jumping. I recall once standing in a queue at a multiplex. I already had my e-tickets, fully paid, and merely had to pick up the printed tickets from the counter. A young man, affluent and educated by all visible reckoning, cut into the queue straight at the window. As one who was at the head of the queue, I directed him to its tail. He politely pleaded with me that he had already purchased the ticket but just had to return some change at the window – the 'I will take very little time' gambit. I chose to fall for it. But as it turned out, the fellow had lied to me through his teeth. He completed his full transaction, namely, bought his tickets, paid the money, took back the change, grinned at me to let me know for sure how smart he had been, and left me looking like a chump!

Yes, such is our social norm – not only jumping queues but also doing it by hook or by crook, or even with outright and in-your-face lies. In a society where queue-jumping is the rule rather than the exception, any iterative game-theoretic plays will suggest that you would be a chump not to jump queues yourself. As a society, we have resolved not to set examples for others. Does this mean we are patient with such brazen queue-jumpers? My take is no; we are fatalistic. We have far too many other, and way more important, battles to fight just for survival. So why bother about this little battle about a lousy queue-jumper? 'In any case, I cannot change the system. So let me live with it' – that's our take. That's why we do not research our behaviour.

Well, Allon and Hanany probably mean well and speak for much of the world, but certainly not for us. No, sir.

But there is more to game theory than we saw in this chapter. Readers' discretion is advised for the next chapter because, as we explore more of game-theoretic situations in real life as played out on our roads, for example, we may find what we see disturbing!

7

The Theory of Queue-jumping
Mid-traffic

A lady was trying to jump the lane in the rush hour traffic in Delhi. A traffic policeman stopped her and asked to see her driving licence.

'Mam', it says here that on account of your weak eye sight, you should be wearing glasses when driving.'

'Well,' replied the lady, 'I have contacts.'

The policeman saluted her and let her go.

Even the ardently patriotic amongst us will not deny that one of our most definitive things as a nation is utterly chaotic traffic. And the traffic presents an important arena for showcasing our queuing abilities (or the lack of them).

It would be instructive here to revisit another game-theoretic situation relating to how traffic jams typically build up.

Game Theory as Played Out on Our Streets

Consider a routine street scene where traffic from an arterial road approaches a bottleneck, as a result of which a queue starts building up at the junction. Let's say I am just joining the tail end of the queue. I have no information on how long it stretches ahead of me and how long I may be held up in it. I now have two alternatives: I either stick to one lane and follow the car in front or I jump lanes and try to steer to the extreme left (or right), using the meagre unpaved pedestrians' passage or obstructing the oncoming traffic in a bid to somehow emerge further ahead in the queue.

Let's say if I maintain lane discipline, the traffic is expected to clear, say, in ten minutes. However, if I jump the queue (while no one else does), I will be out of the jam in half the time.

Thus faced with two alternatives, which one should I opt for?

The answer jumps at me: I should cut the queue, since it involves spending less time in it. This is perfectly rational. Most human beings are selfish – enough for all of them to wish to minimize the time they spend in the queue. Being selfish and being rational are more or less the same. So my decision to jump the queue can hardly be questioned, given that I am selfish and rational.

While this is indeed so, there is only one problem here. Like most folks, I overestimate my own rationality and underestimate that of the others. If jumping the queue to minimize my time in it is the best strategy for me, it must obviously be so for others in the queue as well who are also selfish and rational. And the result is that we have virtually everyone jumping lanes, resulting in the usual mess – a nasty gridlock. And instead of emerging from the jam in ten minutes if one had maintained lane discipline, one remains stuck for an hour.

Mutual and Common Knowledge

Interestingly, while each individual in the jam knows what the 'best strategy' is for him or her *individually* (in mathematics, this is termed as mutual knowledge of the best strategy), they seem to think that they alone are privy to this strategy and act as if they are unaware that all the others are also aware of the same 'best strategy' (what mathematicians call common knowledge)! In other words, while we all have mutual knowledge of the best strategy, we do not have the common knowledge that the best strategy is in fact common knowledge!

In case you are confused how mutual knowledge differs from common knowledge, it is like this:

For people to obey simple traffic rules, like keeping to the left, it is not enough that everyone knows about the rule (meaning, having mutual knowledge about keeping left). Even when all the people know the rule, they may not follow it if they do not simultaneously know that all other road users are also aware of it (there being common knowledge about the rule). Everyone being aware of the rule means there is mutual knowledge of it. But everyone being aware that all (or most) others know about it too is what constitutes common knowledge. Put simply, common knowledge implies that everyone knows – and everyone knows that everyone knows.

If we all knew that everybody knows what the best strategy is and will be jumping lanes, will we be inclined to follow the best strategy? The answer to the question is rather complex, but we will take a shot at it using a variation of the above example.

Game-theoretic Traffic Behaviour

Consider the build-up to a common scene witnessed at our closed railway crossings where motorists refuse to line up one behind the other on their side of the road and instead jump lanes to the right, potentially obstructing traffic that will come from the other side once the crossing is opened.

At first however, a line of vehicles starts building up on both sides of the crossing in an orderly fashion. If both the lines wait calmly in their designated lanes until the gate opens, all the vehicles can cross in about 5 minutes.

Let's say I am just joining the end of the queue on one side when I notice that the road to my right is fairly empty (since that part of it is meant for oncoming vehicles). I am tempted to steer to the right, all the way to the front, close to the gate. My strategy is that as the gate opens I will be among the first to squeeze through to the other side so that I will clear the crossing in, say, half a minute.

One would imagine that the other motorists in the line will discourage me from doing so. But strangely no such thing happens. What instead happens is that I have now opened a 'new lane' and quite a few others line up behind me. If nobody on the other side of the crossing adopts the same 'strategy', let's say the lane-jumpers expect to get across the gate in about 2.5 minutes on average (though, being the first among the queue-jumpers, I probably get across in 0.5 minutes).

But those on the other side of the crossing are no simpletons. They come from the same stock as us. Nevertheless, if good sense miraculously prevails, and they maintain lane discipline, they and the chumps on my own side who stuck to the correct lane will clear the crossing in, say, 10 minutes.

If, on the other hand, those on the opposite side also mimic what happened on my side, there would be a proper logjam, and everybody would probably take 15 minutes to clear the crossing.[1]

Which of the two alternatives should I opt for? The dilemma is not a simple one to resolve; nor is the game-theoretic framework very simple. But we can represent the situation as follows. The pay-off matrix of the situation (in terms of the time spent in the traffic jam and hence indicated in negative numbers) looks like this:

		Drivers on one side	
		Follow lane	Jump lane
Drivers on the other side	Follow lane	-5, 5	-2.5, -10
	Jump lane	-10, -2.5	-15, -15

Traffic Snafus and Traffic Dilemma

Do we recognize the dilemma the situation presents? It certainly looks like the Prisoner's Dilemma. But is it?

Prisoner's Dilemma, first identified by Melvin Dresher and Merill Flood of Rand Corporation in 1950 and subsequently articulated by Albert Tucker in its current form, goes like this: Assume you and I are conspirators in a crime. Both of us are supremely selfish and coldly rational. We are being interrogated in two separate cells and are not allowed to communicate with each other. The interrogator tells you that he has enough circumstantial evidence against each of us to put both of us away in the slammer for two years each. However, if you squeal on me and help him prosecute me, he will let you off right away but give me five years behind bars. He also tells you that he is making an identical offer to me (though you and I cannot communicate). You reflect upon the offer momentarily and ask, 'But what if both of us confess everything?' 'Sorry,' he says, 'in that case I will have to put you both away for four years.'

Assuming that our behaviour is selfish and rational, our responses to the offer are guided by what is in our best self-interest. Emotions such as decency, fairness and graciousness are irrelevant. Our only concern is to get as little time as possible in the slammer.

Now, here is our dilemma: should we squeal on the other?

As rational and intelligent beings, each of us would argue thus: 'If he decides to snitch, it is best if I do too. Why should the scoundrel go scot-free while I get the slammer for five years? On the other hand, if he is naive enough not to snitch, it is in my interest to do so and get away while he lands behind bars.' So no matter what I do, your 'rational' choice is to squeal.

I, on my part, cannot trump that logic either and follow suit. The squeal–squeal decision earns both of us four years in the slammer. But if we had decided not to squeal, we would have served only two years. It is obvious that in order not to squeal, one need not be driven by higher-order values like friendship, kindness or altruism. 'Do not squeal', in fact, turns out to be the better option even if we are supremely selfish and rational, though hardly a convincing one when you are one of the prisoners facing the dilemma.

We all understand immediately (mutual knowledge) that if those on the other side are not going to jump the lane, it is in our best interest to do so, because then we can clear the crossing in a mere 2.5 minutes, while otherwise it could take 10 minutes. On the other hand, if those on the opposite side are going to jump the lane, well, then we are seriously tempted to do so ourselves (why should they get away in 2.5 minutes, leaving us to clear the crossing in take 10 minutes?). As a consequence, both parties end up spending

15 minutes crossing the gate. If only both sides had desisted from jumping lanes, each side would have crossed in five minutes.

So what is the rational thing to do? One may be tempted to answer this question by saying that even when you see others jumping lanes, do not do so yourself, because you would still be better off (at 10 minutes) than if both parties jumped lanes (15 minutes). But then it means letting the lane-jumpers on the opposite side get away scot-free. Should we not pay them in the same coin, even if it costs us an additional 5 minutes (given that law enforcers are not doing their job)? So you are probably as likely to jump the queue as not.

Clearly, it takes only one rotten apple to spoil a good part of an entire basket (and I often feel these are the apples that need to be fined the heaviest since they catalyse bad behaviour), and that is what we observe on our roads – a game-theoretic situation with no clear equilibrium in sight.

The 5 minutes that it would take to clear the crossing if everybody observed lane discipline is the Reward (or R) for sticking to one's lane. The 10 minutes spent by the non-lane-jumper is the Sucker's Pay-off (or S) for not jumping the queue when others did. The 2.5 minutes is the temptation (or T) for the lane-jumper to jump the lane when others do not. And 15 minutes is the penalty (or P) for all when everyone jumps the queue.[2]

For Prisoner's Dilemma to hold, we must have T>R>P>S and (T+S)/2<R. However, in our case, only the second condition is satisfied. For example, -2.5 > -5 > -15 < -10 and

(-2.5-10)/2 < -5, that is, -6.25 < -5 (keeping in mind that the numbers are negative, being time *spent*). The inequality does not meet the requirements of the classic Prisoner's Dilemma and hence does not provide a clear or unique solution to our Traffic Dilemma.

Even if one motorist jumps the lane, demonstration effect leads many others to follow suit. Why should I wait longer only to let the other idiot cross over sooner? On the other hand, why should I cut my nose to spite my face? That is why strict enforcement of traffic discipline becomes the only important imperative but is sadly entirely neglected in our land. So both behaviours – jumping and not jumping the lane – are equally likely, and this is what we often observe.

That's also how traffic snarls occur. We all have the mutual knowledge about what is best for us individually (namely, jumping the queue is better for me individually) but do not have the common knowledge that what's best for me is also best for all others and that all others know it and that all others know that all others know it. 'My time is more important than everybody else's time' is mutual knowledge but not common knowledge!

We seem to love jumping lanes and zigzagging as we overtake except when we are at the receiving end. Perhaps that's why it does not occur to us that our traffic sense needs desperate improvement. And for that to happen, we need mutual as well as common knowledge that if we jump lanes, very likely we will have a huge penalty to pay. Is it possible to bring about such common knowledge? Perhaps through appropriate education. What kind of education can best achieve this?

Influencing the Motorists' Choices

We have all seen in person or on television that in most countries (outside South Asia at least) traffic moves in a far more disciplined manner. Can we possibly educate our domestic motorists to observe lane discipline more often than not?

Yes, we can, to echo Barack Obama's exhortation during his presidential campaign, even if we are bound to sound a tad less optimistic, given the sheer magnitude of the task of educating the multitude! Actually, this is not as difficult as it appears at first.

Skinner's Conditioning

We only need to reconcile ourselves to the fact that the kind of education most suited for the purpose may be no different from what is deployed for training animals. Animals are usually trained by a combination of rewarding the right behaviour and penalizing the wrong one, *à* la the operant conditioning of psychologist B.F. Skinner. Even if this sounds rather crude for modifying certain kinds of abhorrent behaviour, such a strategy may not be misplaced.

For example, when you are educating your dog to fetch that ball that you have chucked, you do not so much penalize him for not chasing the ball or for chasing it, or picking it up and then trotting away from you. You simply wait till he brings the ball and drops it at your feet and then you promptly reward him with a biscuit. When this is done several times over, the dog learns to associate fetching and dropping the ball at your feet with the biscuit. On the other hand, when you are toilet-training the same animal, you penalize him with some whacks when he soils your bed or sofa but do not really reward him for doing it outdoors.

Similarly, reasonable motorists should be steered towards following basic traffic rules, regulations and discipline without any explicit reward, except the implicit reward of enjoying better traffic movement. We call this the self-regulation of motorists. But self-regulation in the total absence of regulation is almost never achievable. That is why we need to condition our motorists to associate bad traffic behaviour with some penalties. This is supposed to be the job of our traffic police (who also need to be similarly trained by being penalized for not doing their job).

Self-regulation Withers without Regulation

Our regulatory mechanism should be such that even a single stray bad motorist has a high probability of being caught, with severe consequences to follow. A high probability of being caught coupled with a severe penalty when caught (like a heavy financial penalty, cancellation of driving licence or steep increase in the insurance premium, etc.) increases the total expected pain from bad traffic behaviour. This should be a relatively simple and even rewarding job for our traffic police, as they can add to their welfare coffers, except that our police are unfortunately preoccupied with 'far more important' things like bandobast duty, VIP duty and morcha duty to be able to devote time to traffic duty.

With such enforcement of regulation almost entirely lacking, little wonder that self-regulation among the populace is conspicuous by its absence, and the ensuing free-for-all ensures that our traffic is perennially in a state of chaos, with people jumping lanes without a worry about being penalized. To come to the point, when the temptation for queue-jumping is high and regulatory disincentive for doing so is low, self-regulation withers away and the incidence of queue-jumping remains high. As if our propensity for queue-jumping weren't good enough, we have a system tailor-made for queue-jumping (in the absence of penalties) that greatly accentuates this already well-developed propensity.

Many of my friends take umbrage at my proclivity to denounce my own countrymen at the honk of a car. They point out to me that traffic snafus aren't uncommon even in the developed world, so what am I complaining about? My response: yes, there are traffic woes the world over, but they don't usually emanate from the idiotic behaviour of motorists who are highly incentivized to be lawless by the lack of even the barest minimum enforcement of regulation.

A little reflection should reveal that the best way to discourage queue-jumping is to disincentivize the temptation to do so through effective measures. As the probability of being brought to book and the cost of being so booked mounts, with steep fines and threats of cancellation of one's licence, etc., the ardour for jumping queues is naturally doused. But without such oversight, no amount of civic sense alone can resist the temptation to jump queues.

At a time when the cost of electronics is falling faster than man in Genesis 3, there is little case for not having more electronic surveillance for more effective traffic policing. Just installing one closed-circuit television camera at every crossing where unruly motorists clog the road and acting on the evidence should discourage much of such behaviour. But for some mysterious reason, we don't do the obvious.

Other obvious measures to dampen motorists' QJP may include unclogging of roads by removing illegal places of worship, cattle and other assorted zoological specimens; speeding up road repairs and different kinds of construction; better coordination between different road-digging agencies; having in place clear signs and signals, and so on. Why should these measures bring down queue-jumping propensity? At present, a queue-jumper may save, say, an extra five or ten minutes by driving on the wrong side of the road. But if better road conditions reduce this differential to, say, only two or three minutes, an average motorist may be more inclined to follow lane discipline.

Many of my well-meaning friends and foes alike frequently point out that the same Indians who drive like maniacs in India develop new personas when transplanted to Dubai, Singapore or Paris. The reason for this transformation should be evident by now. Quite apart from the demonstration effect that we alluded to earlier, it doesn't take long even for our most hardened brethren to realize that 'over there' the regulations are enforced rather diligently. This in turn makes them more inclined to 'self-regulate'.

Transfer of Learning

Elements of traffic management discussed above are also applicable to other kinds of queues. Providing more service windows, quick and efficient automated systems, retractable barriers, yellow lines that separate the queue from the individual being serviced, more space for queues, in-line distractions or entertainment, secondary queues for those with special needs or special tickets, CCTVs to capture unruly behaviour and other similar measures can all help reduce the temptation to jump queues. But these can work only when there is a will to treat unruly queues as a problem. Unfortunately, in our country, no problem is considered worthy of serious attention because there is always a higher-order problem that calls for more urgent attention.

In a more caring world, when designing queues, planners try to make the wait pleasant so as to ensure that the queues remain orderly and there is little incentive to cut in. Businesses and service providers appreciate some basic principles of queuing psychology, which helps fill up empty time, making the wait seem shorter through a variety of ways. In most countries, visitors lining up at theme parks see this principle at work in queues that use smart designs and technology to make the wait itself an entertaining experience.

Efforts have also been made to minimize the length of the queues, though not always with much success. For example, online and self-check-in facilities were introduced at airports in the hope that they would shorten the queues. Nothing of the sort happened. Check-in queues are very much around, and, what is more, there are often impressive lines in front of self-check-in machines! Moreover, even after checking in online, one may still have a bag to drop off, which invariably means another queue! A recent survey in the UK found that queues at baggage drop-off counters are probably just as much of a nuisance as the ones at check-in, with virtually no reduction in the overall waiting time, which remained at about twenty-one minutes.[3]

In our parts, where the government does not consider the common man worthy of even the most basic amenities, it is a bit much to expect ordinary service providers to think of better designs for queues. But we are none the unhappier for this state of affairs. After all, our fatalism has always taught us to lower our expectations rather than rise to them.

Peer Pressure

If you were to jump a queue in London, you would be dead if looks could kill. It is not difficult to imagine that the police in London may be required not so much to prevent one from jumping a queue as to save the queue-jumper from queue rage. There is tremendous social pressure against queue-jumping. You would be politely (though not always) but firmly (always) told where the end of the queue is. So the probability of being caught if you try queue-jumping in London remains high, albeit at a social level. And the cost of queue-jumping also remains very high, albeit mostly in terms of disapproval.

Closer home, as we know, we have little social disapproval for queue-jumping. If anything, it is the objector who feels a subtle sense of social disapproval as he often finds his to be the lone dissenting voice. Our lack of social disapproval for queue-jumping is also because queue-jumpers are usually more numerous than those objecting to them. So it does appear a trifle unseemly to make a fuss over a silly issue, namely, jumping a queue. Mercifully queue rage is not very rampant. But the flip side is that queue-jumping is.

It is now time for some advanced lessons in queue-jumping. Let us move on to the next chapter and learn how we can remain one step ahead in our queue-jumping when we travel overseas.

8

Some Imaginative Cases of Queue-jumping

In the Gulf countries, queues for men and women are typically separate. This helps women in so far as lines for men are usually longer than those for women.

In one of their public offices, a lady was observed wandering about, holding her documents in hand.

An official, trying to be helpful, pointed to the women's queue and told her, 'Stand in that line.'

'I can't. I'm married,' she replied, pointing to a sign that read, 'SINGLES (sic) LINE ONLY.'

People have been devising newer tricks to jump queues all the time. Some are elegant and some not-so-elegant.

The not-so-elegant queue-jumping tactics are often tacky. Consider this. In 2012, the *New York Times* carried a news item headlined, 'Wheelchair Fakers Skip Airport Security Lines.' The essence of the story was that as the security lines at airports were getting interminably longer and slower thanks to heavy security checks, some of the passengers had found an original way to beat the lines. They were requesting for wheelchairs to cut through the long-winding queues. As soon as they were on the other side of the security counters, they would miraculously stand up and walk away, baggage and all. The report did not mention the nationality of these original thinkers.

The *Wall Street Journal* in 2013 termed the phenomenon 'Miracle Wheelchairs'. Some have likened it to men dressing up as women when the Titanic was about to go down so that they could be the first to board the lifeboats!

This strategy works because under the 1986 Air Carrier Access Act in the US, all airlines are required to accommodate disabled travellers (and they do not have to prove their disability) free of charge. It is a surprise that the trick hasn't caught on in India, given that the Airports Authority of India Act also makes a similar provision, calling upon all airlines to provide wheelchairs to anyone who asks for one.

Lest you despair that we may be falling behind other countries when it comes to queue-jumping, columnist Radhika Vaz writing in the *Times of India* refers to a local variant which assures us that our shenanigans are as good as anybody else's.[1] In this gambit, I am a wheelchair-bound passenger. All I have to do is simply ask my attendant to jump the queue at a coffee kiosk on my behalf. All my attendant has to do if challenged is point towards me. And on cue I must wear a suitably dour expression of entitlement.

There are others who play the children card, sending their kids to jump queues while they stay on the sidelines. After all, who is going to challenge eleven- and twelve-year-olds jumping queues? Besides, the strategy has the collateral benefit of starting their training early in life. Nor is the occasional use of the gender card by the fairer sex entirely unknown, even when there are no separate queues for men and women.

The Tough Nut to Crack — Jumping Call Centre Queues

In this department, we are largely a nation of novices. Not that we haven't suffered the double whammy of contacting a call centre when in distress and then being kept on hold interminably. Not only is the experience frustrating, but it can be expensive as well, especially if you are calling from Europe and incurring international roaming charges to notify your bank about the loss of your credit card.

Fortunately for us in India, service providers have at least so far spared us premium helplines (called priority answer services), where you can jump the usual long queues and be connected with a real person faster — as long as you are willing to pay through your nose.

Even seasoned Indian queue-jumpers must have often pulled their hair out at their inability to jump call centre queues and be put through to a human being with a real voice. But help is at hand from a messiah of sorts.

Don't Get Mad; Get Ahead

Travel site Kayak.com's Paul English, a computer hacker-turned-guru for call centre queue-jumpers, provides every kind of help you need to jump online queues, though his tips are essentially meant for British and American systems. But many of them should serve us well too.

For instance, one simple trick he tells callers to try is to repeatedly press a single button, which helps them evade the automatic call answering systems. In no time at all, they will find themselves connected to a human voice ready to handle their complaint.

Of course, beating the queue in this world is more nuanced than in the physical one. For example, he discloses that Orange users calling the mobile company's call centre should enter some random cell numbers instead of their own when prompted. They can be almost certain of being connected to an operator who will handle the complaint directly.

Paul's algorithms to beat call centres are called his cheat sheets. They are a free service which help callers reach humans to complain to in some 175 corporates and institutions, which include companies in the fields of finance, insurance, pharmaceuticals, telecommunication, manufacturing, retail, shipping, travel, technology, and television and satellite companies. He also has cheat sheets in the making for most of the Fortune 100 companies.

Paul English's IVR cheat sheet lists the companies alphabetically, providing against each the phone numbers the clients are advised to call and the 'Steps to find a human'. These may include 'Press 0 or choose "member services" for a company', or 'Press 0 repeatedly for a second company', or 'Press 00', or 'Directly dial the given (by the cheat sheet) executive office number for a third company', or 'Dial 0000 for the fourth company' and so on.[2]

Even as Paul has been painstakingly working on verifying the many cheat sheets, he has also been receiving online contributions, which are all verified and put on the web.

Perhaps here is an opportunity for our home-grown IT buffs to contribute to some socially useful line-jumping. And I don't mean socially useful in the same sense as Allon and Hanany. Let me explain myself.

We all realize that in the name of call centres, most corporates and even government institutions happily seem to be distancing themselves from irate customers. Not that in India we needed the excuse of call centres for such distancing, but with this additional layer, the service levels are going from bad to worse, because the organizations no longer have to directly deal with angry customers.

Take most of our telecom service providers, especially the private ones. I have noticed – and I have a systematic record of the fact – that every time I go abroad, when on international roaming, I receive several SMSes which repeat themselves as many as twenty times! And what is worse, upon my return when in due course I receive my monthly bill, I find that all the SMSes have been billed to me at a hefty rate of some Rs 6 per SMS. Even in the worst-case scenario, they have nothing to lose and everything to gain, since when you dispute the bill, all they have to do is correct the 'error' and appear gracious in the process.

(I have noticed the best of restaurants, especially those at five-star hotels, doing something similar. Ever so often, when you have been dining out with friends, you find a couple of items – or an extra bottle of wine, if the gathering was particularly large – added to the bill. In most cases, since we do not consider it elegant to check our bills when accompanied with guests, the ruse works. And if you happen to catch the 'error', all they have to do is apologize profusely for the 'inconvenience' caused! Only recently did I learn the reason for this. It seems many politicians, bureaucrats and senior police officials visit these hotels with families and friends for free lunches or dinners. So how do the hotels make up for their losses? By overcharging suckers like you and me, perhaps.)

Most customers, especially corporate ones, end up paying such bills. But the likes of me who make a point of disputing them can have their problem resolved ultimately (with some luck) – but not without those long waits at call centres!

Nor is this an isolated example. Our mobile phone calls drop repeatedly, forcing us to call twice, thrice or even four times to complete our conversation with that one person. This is clearly because the lines of these 'service providers' are terribly overcrowded – the telecom equivalent of a bus designed to carry 50 passengers ferrying 150. And what are the consequences the companies face? None. In fact, they have an incentive not to fix the problem. Why should they when it suits them to earn revenues for two, three or four calls when one would have sufficed?

Don't get me wrong; I am not trying to target the telecom

companies or single them out for shortchanging customers. But do you see any irony in the fact that it was EE – a British telecom giant that services some 28 million customers through T-Mobile, Orange and 4G EE brands – that first introduced a priority answer service? Now, no matter how poor your service, you will only rake in more moolah as complaints mount across the industry and queues become longer and people are driven to use the premium service! A beautiful arrangement!

That call centres shield companies is evident from the account of a retired BBC reporter from Sunderland.[3] Apparently, when he called his bank to find out if he had left his spectacles on the counter of a branch, he was first asked his mother's maiden name and the rest of his vitae before being connected to a call centre lady in Kuala Lumpur. She could not give him the phone number of the branch concerned. Finally, when he found the number on an old letter from the branch and called up, the official demanded to know how he had obtained the number. Had the call centre given it away, someone was going to be in deep trouble.

It is only when companies face more pressure from complaining customers that they are likely to be a touch more responsive. And these cheat sheets help in that direction. Hence my clarion call to my fellow citizens to create India-centric cheat sheets!

But coming back to Paul English, he is reported to have said, 'It has been amazing. My cheat sheet has become so popular that I need someone who can verify at least ten cheats per hour.'[4]

Readers and irate customers have been sharing their own painful call centre stories with him, asking for an end to extortionist 0870 numbers (for 'premium' service), which are known to charge customers up to $0.10 (or Rs 6) per minute. More often than not, customers want to complain about the overcharging of 0870 calls themselves!

What EE Could Have Done Right

What's wrong in having a premium service that helps you jump queues at a price, you may ask. After all, aren't the premium class air travellers doing precisely that?

Yes, but there is a difference. It is not that there was no demand for a service that allowed for a faster route through the long queues at call centres. There was. But the customers of EE were displeased with the sheer crassness with which the scheme was implemented.

EE probably wouldn't have lost goodwill had it implemented the priority answer service as a 'premium service package', under which its customers would have the choice to sign up for faster service for, say, an additional monthly charge, which entitled them to dial a specific customer service number. Such packages that offer various special and faster services already exist and do work well in many industries. But a charge directly linked to a fast-track call-centre sucks.

Hence, paid queue-jumping needs to be handled with care.

Queue-jumping by Tinkering with Algorithms

Imagine you and I are in queue for campus housing allotment at the university where we work, and the demand

1	2	3	4	5	6	7
Parameters	Weights	Ranking Scale: 1 to 3 (3 being most valuable)	Ranking Score		Weighted Average Score	
			You	I	You	I
Qualifications	0.25	PhDs from top institutions = 3 Other PhDs = 2 Non PhDs =1	3	1	0.75	0.25
Seniority in Profession	0.15	More than 15 years = 3 Between 7 and 15 years = 2 Less than 7 years = 1	1	2	0.15	0.30
Date of Joining	0.20	Joined more than 7 years ago = 3 Joined between 3 and 7 years ago = 2 Joined less than 3 years ago = 1	1	2	0.20	0.40
Publications	0.25	More than 15 peer-reviewed publications = 3 Between 7 and 15 = 2 Less than 7 = 1	2	3	0.5	0.75
Department	0.15	Physics, Chemistry, Zoology = 3 Biology, Botany and Anthropology = 2 Others = 1	3	2	0.45	0.3
Total	**1.00**				**2.05**	**2.00**

for housing outstrips availability. Say the university has a policy of deciding our position in the queue based on some algorithm – the algorithm being a function of various parameters, with each one being ascribed a rating and a weight. The parameters our hypothetical university uses are shown in the table above (Column 1), namely, educational qualifications (whether or not the faculty has a PhD, which university the PhD is from, etc.); seniority in the profession (the number of years put in as an academic); date of joining the university (seniority in the university); publications (number of refereed publications); and the department in which we work (whether physics, chemistry, botany, etc.). Let's say the university ranks each faculty member on a three-point scale on these parameters and then ascribes weights to the parameters depending on the kind of faculty they wish to attract or retain at any point of time. For example, currently the university may be specifically looking to attract or retain faculty with outstanding research records and top-quality academic qualifications. Hence they might decide on higher weights for research and academic qualifications (25 per cent each).

The relative weights for various parameters are as indicated in Column 2. Let's say we are both ranked on these parameters in accordance with the criteria indicated in Column 3 and given ranks as shown in Columns 4 and 5. Given the above ranking scores, our weighted average scores for each parameter and the total score are shown in Columns 6 and 7.

The total of the weighted scores shows that you rank

above me as your weighted average score at 2.05 is higher than mine at 2.00. Now let's suppose I am a favourite of the vice-chancellor. How can he ensure that I jump over you (or some others) in the queue?

All he has to do is call a senate meeting (where the members are completely unaware of the subtle manipulation the good VC is doing for my benefit) and suggest a slight change in the policy (algorithm) 'for the betterment of the institution', stating that publications are a tad more important than mere academic qualification and that the weights should be changed from 25 per cent to 20 per cent for qualifications and from 25 per cent to 30 per cent for publications. This results in a total weighted average score of 2.10 for me and 2.00 for you.

Well, I have jumped the housing queue over you smoothly, with some help from the good VC, his reputation intact. And what is more, nobody can call me a queue-jumper!

It is time now for us to move on to more professional queue-jumping.

9

Professional Queuers and Queue-jumping

In a busy airport, there were several aircraft in a long queue for take-off. As the frustration of the wait began to build up, a young pilot spoke into the transmitter, 'I'm bloody bored waiting!'

Ground Traffic Control barked, 'Last aircraft transmitting, identify yourself immediately!'

'You mean you don't have my coordinates?'

'If I had, why the heck would I call for identification?' came the rejoinder.

The young pilot responded, 'I said I was bloody bored, not bloody stupid!'

The basic idea of paying someone to stand as your proxy in a queue is neither terribly original nor new. Many of us have, at one time or the other, paid someone to line up on our behalf at a railway reservation counter or at the American embassy. But these efforts can at best be described as jugaad – an ad hoc way to address the queuing problem. They never evolved into a full-time entrepreneurial venture, leave alone a full-fledged corporate business, even if not listed on the stock exchange – as is the case in some other places.

The Chinese have been outsourcing their queuing for a while now. All those tens of thousands of people lining up for days on end to apply for low-income housing in Xian or for a kindergarten school in Changping have been known to routinely employ professional queuers. In 2011, the National Public Radio (NPR) referred to a certain twenty-eight-year-old Li Qicai, for example, who had made a career out of waiting in queues for a fee. He was doing well enough to employ four more full-time queuers and a host of part-timers. He was charging about $3 per hour.[1]

Good old Europe has been catching up too. In 2014, the economic crisis in Italy created two major challenges: huge unemployment and long queues for most government interactions. A piece in the *Guardian* informs us that when an Italian gentleman by the name of Giovanni Cafaro lost his job in Milan with a clothing firm, he sent out his resume to hundreds of potential employers, but drew a blank. Aware of the impossibly slow bureaucracy of the Italian government, especially at property tax offices, he decided to plunge into entrepreneurship. He became a professional queuer.[2]

But he was way ahead of the Chinese. He charged €10 per hour (almost four times Li's rate) and his business was thriving at the time of writing these lines. He was thinking of setting up a professional agency as he had started receiving requests from Rimini, Naples and La Spezia.

Formalized Fast-tracking of Queues

Organized businesses built around queuing may not be common, but organized fast-tracking of queues is not uncommon. For example, Michael Sandel colourfully describes in his book *What Money Can't Buy* how several states across the US in the 1980s gave car-poolers access to express lanes, which enabled them to travel quicker. There were always some who used professional 'companions', who were paid to accompany them so that they could avail of the benefits. And, of course, there were the imaginative few who would put an appropriately dressed-up human-sized inflated doll in the passenger seat to hoodwink the police and escape the long lines of cars in the standard lanes.[3]

Today, the system has been tweaked in many US cities like Denver, Houston, Miami, Seattle and San Francisco among others to allow even solo drivers to travel in the express lanes meant for car-poolers, for a charge of $10 or so.

Formalized Fast-tracking of Queues Indian Style

We, of course, have our own version of formalized fast-tracking, called the VIP passage. If you are wondering why the populace does not protest against this kind of blatant queue-jumping, the reason may have something to do with our high Power Distance Index (PDI – something we probably share with China). Gerard Hendrik Hofstede, a Dutch researcher, uses PDI to study different cultures.[4] It measures 'the extent to which the less powerful members of organizations and institutions (like in a family or a business) accept and expect that power is distributed unequally'. The higher the acceptance and expectation of power inequality, the higher the 'power distance'.[5]

Given our feudal and servile history, we have reconciled ourselves to the fact that in Mother Nature's ovarian lottery, not all are born equal. Some are indeed so exalted – like politicians, bureaucrats, the rich and the famous, and their kin and kith – that they may not be questioned by lesser mortals when they jump queues.

Miffed by this kind of queue-jumping, I once registered my protest not merely by writing articles in newspapers and blogging against the practice but also by exhorting people to honk in unison every time a full-of-himself VIP zipped through traffic, keeping the rest of us waiting. But some civic-minded worthies wrote in to say how this would contribute to noise pollution!

Professional Queuers

Sandel in his aforementioned book narrates the case of a New York theatre company which puts up a free performance in Central Park every summer for the common man.[6] Apparently, while the free tickets for the evening are made available in the afternoon, the line starts building up hours ahead. Many common people do want to catch the free play but do not have the time to stand in line for hours. As a consequence, an informal little industry has come up in which retired people, the homeless and courier guys offer to stand in the queue for a fee. Before long, the proxies were advertising their services, and, in some cases, were able to charge $125 per ticket for the performance which itself is free.

Demand for line-standers is not restricted to New York. Sandel also refers to Washington, DC, where congressional committees hold hearings for which they reserve some free seats for the media and the general public.[7] These are meant to be given on an FCFS basis. The wait in the queues for these seats can last well over a day. As a consequence, professional queuers often sell positions in these lines to lobbyists, lawyers or corporate honchos for a couple of thousand dollars. For these gentlemen, who walk in at the last moment with their Louis Vuitton briefcases and in pin-striped suits and who have business interests in attending the hearings, $2,000 is loose change.

Not surprisingly, the US market has thrown up a few line-standing companies, including one known as LineStanding. com, which offers line-standers for an hourly fee.

China has something similar in a different context. Doctors' appointments are often difficult to get, and the appointment tickets, though priced at only about $2, may involve waiting in enormously long lines. And this is where the professional queuers step in.

Queues and Black Market

A black marketeer or a ticket scalper of the kind we witness at the first-day, first-show of a Rajinikanth release provides a similar service by lining up in advance for tickets in long queues and then selling them at a premium. In our land, even a rendezvous with God is not free of such scalping, as many who have experienced long lines outside popular temples will testify.

If you think about it, how is ticket scalping or black marketing different from professional queuing? The difference seems to rest on two points. One, in black marketing, the queuers and their proxies are not in a one-to-one relationship, while in professional queuing they are. Two, the black marketeers are seen to be increasing the demand and supply gap, while professional queuers charge only for their time.

Fairness and Morality of Paid Fast-tracking

The above examples of formal fast-tracking, professional queuing and scalping raise some questions: How fair is paying someone to be one's proxy in a queue? How fair is it for a professional queuer to stand in for somebody for a fee? What is wrong if he charges a fee for the effort he puts in by waiting in conditions of sun, rain or snow? Why should his time not have an opportunity cost, considering he could have used it doing something else? Sandel tries to answer such questions as well.[8]

Most economists would argue that there is absolutely nothing wrong in paying others to stand in queues. They call it a free market economy, bringing about more efficient utilization of labour so that there can be little objection to the professional line-standing industry, or for that matter even ticket scalping (its legality apart). After all, aren't individual freedom and maximizing welfare the very foundations of a just society? If a man is down and out and wishes to make a living line-standing for someone who is too busy to do it himself, isn't the transaction strictly a business deal between the two? And what is more, doesn't it maximize the utility for both parties? So what exactly is wrong with this?

The grey nature of the problem is best appreciated through the theatre example Sandel presents in his book. The theatre company's idea was to offer a free service to the common people who could casually walk in and see the play for free. Their show wasn't meant for the affluent citizens who could afford to pay $125 per ticket! Nor was it meant to enable middlemen to make money, which the company itself could easily have earned had it chosen to charge for the tickets. As it turns out, the theatre group in New York did try to discourage proxy queuers.

Why should it do so? After all, no one is engaged in anything illegal. The deal is a win-win for everybody. The line-standers make some money. The citizen is willing to pay for the comfort of not having to stand in line for hours, and, what is more, he shows his keenness to see the play by putting his money on the line.

That last sentence may lead us to the question: is money the best measure of one's keenness? It is when, of two individuals with equal pay, one is willing to shell out more than the other. But it is not when one is more affluent than the other. Nor when one has more pressing demands on his meagre monetary resources, like food or education.

And that is why fast-tracking of queues is really a form of queue-jumping that can be questioned on moral grounds. It militates against the assumption of an egalitarian society.

Could it be that some forms of fast-tracking are somewhat more acceptable than others? Maybe. But critics argue that most such systems relegate the have-nots to the end of the queue while the affluent take advantage of the public service at the cost of the poor.

Does it then mean that if the services are to be genuinely free, the intended beneficiaries must themselves line up for hours? And what would we say if a pregnant woman preferred to pay a tout rather than stand for six hours in a queue? Isn't the professional queuer then rendering a genuine service? Not necessarily.

This is because nothing prevents the service provider from giving priority or preference to the more needy. I recall an instance when my seventy-year-old aunt visiting Paris was stuck in a serpentine queue outside the Palais de l'Elysée (the French presidential palace) on a day when entry happened to be free. She stood quietly in the cold wind, her shawl wrapped tight around her, when a cop appeared by her side, gently held her by her elbow and escorted her to the front of the queue along with her son.

Happy India

Scholars, thinkers and the general public in the West are starting to ask nuanced questions like the ones raised above. Fortunately or unfortunately for us in this part of the world, such questions are hardly troubling, as queue-jumping is a perfectly acceptable phenomenon. Perhaps it suits the larger designs of the ruling classes, even seven decades after Independence, to ensure that a great majority of the countrymen remain mired in illiteracy and poverty so that the PDI remains high.

In any case, what could possibly be the value of a discussion on whether or not paying line-standers is fair or ethical when millions of people face the everyday unfairness of being denied equal opportunities in education, health, employment or pretty much in any sphere of life?

Now that we have seen how professional queuing can be viewed as a form of queue-jumping and is hence unfair, let us look at situations of implicit queue-jumping in the absence of explicit queue-jumpers, throwing up some subtle ethical considerations.

10

Ethics of Queue-jumping for the Scrupulous

Children were lined up in the cafeteria of a Catholic elementary school for lunch. At the head of the table was a large pile of apples.

A nun wrote out a note and posted it on the apple tray: 'Take only ONE. God is watching.'

Moving further along the lunch line, at the other end of the table was a large pile of chocolate chip cookies.

A child whispered aloud, 'Take all you want. God is watching the apples.'

In the preceding section, we discussed how scalpers and professional queuers violate the egalitarianism of queues.

Let us now take a closer look at the queue for the free darshan at Tirupati which the temple authorities offer to the common man. Let us say you are one of those in the queue. Suppose a black marketeer approaches you and offers you a place nearer the head of the queue for Rs 500. Would you take it? You probably experience some inner turmoil irrespective of whether you accept the offer. You are briefly tempted, but the 'disgust' of engaging in a black market transaction to jump the queue, that too at a temple, makes you reconsider.

But what if the person had approached you with the explanation that he and his brother took turns standing in the queue overnight, foregoing their daily wages elsewhere, and hence the charge? The person suddenly transforms from a black marketeer to a professional queuer, and the acceptability of the proposition increases somewhat. Chances are you are a little more comfortable paying the person to jump the queue.

What if the proxy in the queue is one of your own close friends or a member of the family and there is no charge involved? Suddenly the proxy becomes far more acceptable not only to you but to society at large.

Why?

The money factor somehow defiles the idea of equality and fairness. One realizes that the temple authorities (or the theatre group we discussed in the last chapter) could well eliminate the middlemen by directly charging a fast-tracking fee. The added revenue could help the temple increase its philanthropic activities (or the artistes of the theatre group to earn a little extra). But jumping queues with the help of professional queuers and black marketeers merely encourages an industry built on idleness, which adds relatively little value to society and is biased against the least affluent.

Of course, something else troubles us as well. Tirupati temple authorities (and several others) do have fast-track darshans for Rs 2,000, Rs 5,000 and so on. But did the good lord mean his people from different walks of life to have differential access to his darshan? One may argue that those who are willing to pay to jump a queue are those who are keener to get the darshan. Is it immoral to put their money where their keenness is?

That takes us back to the question of money as a measure of every sentiment. Clearly, keenness, when people's financial situations vary considerably, cannot be measured in monetary terms.

And where there is violation of fairness, there is bound to be violation of ethical values.

Ethics of Implicit Queue-jumping

I recall reading an article in the Kellogg School of Management's online journal (*The Operations Room*)[1]. The article presented a situation somewhat as follows:

Imagine a long, formal but virtual queue at a travel desk, where everybody is expected to take a token number and await their turn in the hall. One may seat oneself randomly and approach the service counter as and when the number is called. Let's say I have just entered, taken my token and sat down. The token indicates my position to be twenty-third in the line. A lady seated next to me turns around and tells me within everybody's earshot that she is third in the line, that for some reason she can no longer stay and that I can use her token.

You can bet that I will simply thank Lady Luck incarnate, avail of the good fortune and think no more of the matter. But if you also happen to be in the line with a position well ahead of mine, say, tenth, would you not wonder if it was ethically correct of me to take her token? Would you not feel wronged?

What about the question: 'Is it ethical of the lady to give me the token?' Are the two questions symmetrical? At first, they appear to be so, until you figure that it would have been way easier for the lady to just chuck that token into the dustbin than it would be for me to reject it. My behaviour, more than the lady's, falls within the framework of ethics.

To be honest, I had no intention to cut the line. I *am* cutting no line. I am not even trying to short-circuit the system. For all you know, I may even genuinely agree with you that outright cutting of lines is rude and unfair. But the fact is the lady doesn't want to stay; I never asked or angled for her position; it is simply my good luck that she is giving me her place; I can complete my business in a few minutes rather than wait a couple of hours; and nobody is any the worse than if the lady had stayed on. If so, where am I violating any ethical considerations?

But let's take a second look at the situation. The transaction can be said to have violated the fundamental FCFS principle of queues. What is more, the departure of that lady could have shortened the waiting time of each of those ahead of me by a few minutes. Also, it is quite possible that someone else – like a pregnant mother or an octogenarian – was way more deserving of that token than me.

But who is more deserving? A mother with a small baby in her arms or a seven-month pregnant woman? Or an ageing war veteran with a missing leg? And what about the fund manager who probably has the highest opportunity cost of time and who, if he saves a few minutes, may earn a tad more for scores of investors, ultimately benefiting thousands of retirees as well as the tax coffers?

Let us assume that the average service time in our context is 10 minutes. Let us also assume that on average the cost of waiting in the queue is Rs 2 per minute. When I jump from the twenty-third to the third position, I save Rs 400 (20 x 10 x 2). In other words, I profit at the cost of others.

For a strictly ethical person, when you remove the fig leaf, accepting the token does amount to cutting the line, which in turn means tampering with the FCFS system that is designed for fairness and to make the queuers' lives better.

Naturalists who frequent the African savannah would appreciate this aspect of tampering. These naturalists witness situations such as a leopard attacking a newly born gazelle, or a crocodile stealthily approaching a baby hippo, or a pack of hyenas attaching a sick but majestic lion. The rules of the jungle dictate that the naturalist refrain from interfering with nature at all costs and not try to save the baby gazelle, hippo calf or the lion. Let nature take its course. So perhaps the lady and I should both just let nature take its course and not tamper with the social system of queues and not give away the token to anybody or accept it from anyone.

Ethics of Queue-jumping in Health Care Systems

Ethical considerations also arise when medical professionals permit preferential access to publicly funded (and sometimes even privately funded) health care. By definition, preferential access to health care – a professional term for queue-jumping – is nothing but access to care based on factors that are extraneous to medical need and ethical fairness. Preferential access may be permitted due to nepotism, influence, power, money, recommendations from professional colleagues or referrals.

Consider a hospital that has a queue of patients awaiting a kidney donor for transplant. However fair this queue may or may not be, a surgeon employed in the hospital may decide to favour a patient who is a relative, or a friend, or someone referred by a former teacher, or recommended by his banker who is giving him a large home loan and so on, especially if the criteria of the waiting list allows enough leeway for his 'interpretation'. Our first impulse is often to do the best for ourselves, especially if we regard a position not as one meant to serve but as one of power. And then it is easy to forget that when we seek an advantage for someone close to us, we are short-changing someone not close to us.

Or consider this. You are in charge of emergency care in a government hospital. An obviously destitute man in a coma is brought in. He has been involved in a serious accident and is going to need much of the rare blood group available in the hospital. Within minutes, the comatose son of the cabinet secretary is brought in with serious injuries from a motorcycle accident. He too belongs to the same rare blood group. You are permitted to accept the more serious cases ahead of the less serious ones. The hospital's stated policy is FCFS. However, under severe pressure from the cabinet secretary, will you bump his son up the queue? But here you have two cases that look equally bad. What do you do?

What about the hypothetical medical director of a hospital who, for the sake of much-needed funds for the institute, diverts some of the organs received from the Organ Retrieval Banking Organization (of the All India Institute of Medical Sciences, Delhi) to paying customers ahead of non-paying ones?

Examples of such queue-jumping could be varied, many and complex. They could be blatantly unfair or go into ethical grey areas. They could be couched in professional courtesies or portrayed as deviations from the norm for the 'greater good'. Sometimes the conflict of interest may be such that one does not even know whether or not one is consciously tilting the balance in someone's favour.

In a preferential access enquiry in Calgary, Alberta, Canada, a knee surgeon testified that he feels 'conflicted when friends or associates ask for treatment' but said that, like many other doctors, he will see that person after office hours to avoid bumping anyone else out of the line. According to the surgeon, 'queue-jumping occurs all the time because Alberta's health care is so broken that people with connections will naturally do whatever they can to get timely help.'[2] Sounds despairingly similar to India's health care system.

We the People versus Queuing Ethics

Forgive me if my reference to the ethics of queue-jumping sounds somewhat facetious when I am still struggling with the basics of fairness, decency, respect and concern for others in my everyday life. I am still trying to figure out why ethical considerations – even in larger issues that impact our lives, leave alone petty queue-jumping – entirely bypass me, notwithstanding my frequent reminder to myself of our glorious and rich heritage.

Given everything that seems obviously wrong with my civic behaviour, why do I find it difficult to borrow the best of Western culture which, in the last fifty to hundred years seems to have come a very long way? It may be that until a couple of centuries ago, many of those cultures thought nothing of marching into other people's territories, killing them, maiming them and taking away their riches, while we remained a pacifist people. Until a hundred years ago, many of them widely practised slavery. Until a few decades ago, many of these societies did not have universal suffrage for women, who were treated as chattels, while in ancient India women were treated with respect. In our worldview, these were societies of hunter-gatherers at a time when we were gifting esoteric mathematical nuggets to the world. Our cultural heritage goes back 5,000 years while much of theirs is probably way more recent.

And yet, despite the stark contrast between our societies, today I would be blind not to notice their orderliness, cleanliness, work culture, hunger for knowledge, civic sense, ability to administer themselves and their wealth creation vis-à-vis ours. There is a virtual absence in us of all that is inherent in them today. And yet, it never seems to hit us hard where it should. Our so-called leaders are content exhorting our youth to eschew what they derisively refer to as 'Western culture'. In our view, all is well with our culture; it is other cultures that have all the problems.

As I said earlier in the book, if we are ever to find solutions, we first need to recognize that we have problems. We need to ask ourselves whether we are citizens of the twenty-first century; whether we are worthy descendants of a great and ancient civilization. But rather than ask such questions, we are quick to point to the warts in other cultures, as if they justify the cancerous tumour of apathy and boorishness in ours. Are we given to justifying our low benchmarks lest we have to work hard to raise them – which would of course be too much trouble? I am still wondering.

Epilogue

Queue-jumping in India is a troubling social phenomenon, made alarmingly ugly by the total refusal of service providers, regulators and society alike to apply their minds. It is never on our list of foremost concerns to address. But queue-jumping is only a symptom of our larger social apathy, corrupted mindset, the wide gap between the powerful and the common folk, our innate indifference to fairness and concern for others, and the complete denial that we have a problem in the first place. It is a problem symptomatic of deeper ones so that it appears queue-jumping is going to be around for a very long time.

Most of our institutions do little to enforce systems and processes to honour the integrity of queues for the services they provide. A few like the IITs and IIMs have shown that it is possible to maintain such integrity after all through appropriate internal systems and processes. So jump-proof are their waiting lists that they can withstand VVIP pressures of the highest order and simply cannot be tampered with. Over the years, VVIPs have learnt this lesson, and rarely, if ever, even try to approach these institutes with requests to accommodate their offspring. As the regulation strengthened, self-regulation took care of itself.

A weak regulatory system encourages queue-jumping in all formats, which in turn makes the enforcement of measures to curb queue-jumping increasingly more difficult. This clearly implies that first and foremost we need to recognize that queue-jumping, especially in a country where queues are an important social reality, is a problem worthy of being tackled. The best way to do this is to employ software, gadgets such as cameras and fool-proof electronic systems and processes to enforce queuing discipline.

For example, e-ticketing to a large extent addressed the challenges of queuing and queue-jumping for railway reservations, making the common man's life infinitely better. Also, CCTVs can help curb serious traffic and queue-jumping cases. Transparent and tamper-proof computerized waitlists in educational or other institutions can significantly reduce queue-jumping by power brokers.

Fairness and concern for others do not come naturally to us and so we, neither the clerk at the lowest level nor the head of an institution at the highest level, have ever looked at our queue-jumping propensity as a malady that needs fixing. It's high time we stopped seeking comfort in that age-old adage – 'We are like this only!' – and faced up to a problem which, if addressed, can lead to a more just society.

Notes

1. The Wisdom of Queues

1. 'Archaeological evidence suggests Chinese people "once queued",' China Daily Show, 18 April 2014, Lao Shouxing, http://chinadailyshow.com/archaeological-evidence-suggests-chinese-people-once-queued/, accessed 2 September 2014.

2. The 'Java man' was a group of fossils found by Dutch physician Eugene Dubois in the Dutch East Indies.

3. V. Raghunathan, *Games Indians Play* (New Delhi: Penguin Books India, 2006).

2. The Sociology of Queues across Nations

1. 'Archaeological evidence suggests Chinese people "once queued",' China Daily Show, 18 April 2014, Lao Shouxing, http://chinadailyshow.com/archaeological-evidence-suggests-chinese-people-once-queued/, accessed 2 September 2014.

2. Ibid.

3. Timothy Tang, 'In defence of Singapore's "Kiasu" queuers,' http://www.mumbrella.asia/2014/04/defence-singapores-kiasu-queuers/, accessed 18 April 2016.

4. 'Case Study: Medicare Australia,' Nexa.com – Australia's

leading customer experience specialist, http://nexa.com.au/portfolio-item/medicare-australia/, accessed 18 April 2016.

5. See https://www.youtube.com/watch?v=89_soJefAQ, accessed 27 December 2014.

6. Peter C. Newman, *Here Be Dragons: Telling Tales of People, Passion and Power* (Toronto: A Douglas Gibson Book, 2004): 684

7. Don Norman, 'The Psychology of Waiting Lines,' http://www.jnd.org, 21 August 2008. Subsequently published as 'Designing Waits That Work,' MIT Sloan Management Review (1 July 2009).

8. Rodney Bolt, *Xenophobes' Guide to the Dutch*, Chapter 7, Kindle edition, 2008.

9. 'Italy Answers,' *Italy Magazine*, 26 May 2009, http://www.italymagazine.com/community/post/italian-queuing-system, accessed 18 April 2016.

10. 'Germany's hyperinflation-phobia,' *Economist*, 15 November 2013.

11. If you are keen, you can even buy a note on e-bay (http://www.ebay.com/bhp/b-pengo).

12. See http://worldlibrary.org/articles/hyperinflation, accessed on 18 April 2016.

13. Vladimir Sorokin, 'Words without Borders,' published as an afterword to the new edition of *The Queue* (New York: New York Review Books, 2008).

14. Ibid.

15. George Aiyetty, 'Opinion: What Ghana can teach the rest of Africa about democracy,' CNN, 6 December 2012, http://edition.cnn.com/2012/12/06/opinion/ghana-elections-george-ayittey/, accessed 18 April 2016.

16. By 'Western' I mean the world west of, say, the meridian drawn though Istanbul.

3. The Physiology of Queues

1. 'Why Waiting Is Torture,' *New York Times*, 18 August 2012, http://www.nytimes.com/2012/08/19/opinion/sunday/why-waiting-in-line-is-torture.html?pagewanted=all&_r=0, accessed 4 May 2016.
2. Remember, 'well-dressed person' is a relative term here – relative to the utterly wretched pedestrian or cyclist.
3. Hans Wiktorsson and Jan Tind Sørensen, 'Implications of automatic milking on animal welfare,' *Automatic Milking: A Better Understanding* (The Netherlands: Wageningen Academic Publishers, 2004): 371-81.
4. Susan C. Alberts, Heather E. Watts and Jeanne Altmann, 'Queuing and queue-jumping: Long-term patterns of reproductive skew in male savannah baboons, Papio cynocephalus,' *Animal Behaviour*, 65.4 (2003): 821-40.
5. Richard H. Thaler, *The Winner's Curse: Paradoxes and Anomalies of Economic Life* (New Jersey: Princeton University Press, 1994): 3.

4. The Psychology of Queues

1. Evert Gummeson, *Total Relationship Marketing* (Chennai: Macmillan, 2008): 71.
2. Comment submitted by Sassy Velociraptor on Reddit: 'Tales from Retail.' See http://www.reddit.com/r/TalesFromRetail/comments/1koped/the_best_way_to_deal_with_queuejumpers/, accessed 2 January 2015.
3. 'Cherie Blair Spares Violent Queue Rage Thug Because He Is a Religious Man,' *Mail Online*, 4 February 2010, http://www.dailymail.co.uk/news/article-1245506/Cherie-Blair-spares-violent-queue-rage-thug-religious-man.html, accessed 28 April 2016.

4. 'Murder at the Checkout: Shopkeeper Killed in Sainsbury's after Queue-jumping Row,' Mail Online, 12 June 2008, http://www.dailymail.co.uk/news/article-1025855/Murder-checkout-Shopper-killed-Sainsburys-queue-jumping-row.html, accessed 28 April 2016.

5. 'Is This Justice – Five Years for Ruining a Life?' *Telegraph*, 1 February 2004, http://www.telegraph.co.uk/news/uknews/1453188/Is-this-justice-five-years-for-ruining-a-life.html, accessed 28 April 2016.

6. David Maister, 'The Psychology of Waiting Lines,' Harvard Business School Teaching Note 9-684-064, 1985, http://davidmaister.com/articles/the-psychology-of-waiting-lines/, accessed 9 July 2014.

7. W.E. Sasser, J. Olsen and D.D. Wyckoff, *Management of Service Operations*: Text, Cases and Readings (New York: Allyn and Bacon, 1979).

8. Christopher Lovelock, Jochen Wirtz and Jayanta Chatterjee, *Services Marketing: People, Technology, Strategy – A South Asian Perspective* (Delhi: Dorling Kindersley, 2009): 260.

9. A. Pawlowski, 'Queuing psychology: Can waiting in line be fun?' CNN International, 20 November 2008, http://edition.cnn.com/2008/TECH/science/11/20/queuing.psychology/index.html?_s=PM:TECH, accessed 2 September 2014.

5. *Useful Lessons in Effective Queue-jumping*

1. S. Milgram, H.J. Libety, R. Toledo and J. Wackenhut, 'Response to Intrusion into Waiting Lines,' *Journal of Personality of Social Psychology*, Vol. 51, No. 4 (1986): 683-89.

2. E. Langer, A. Blank and B. Chanowitz, 'The mindlessness of ostensibly thoughtful action: The role of "placebic" information in interpersonal interaction,' *Journal of*

Personality and Social Psychology, Vol. 36, No. 6 (1978): 635-42.

3. Robert B. Cialdini, *Influence: The Psychology of Persuasion* (New York: Collins Business, 2007): 4.

4. 'Murder at National Service camp,' *The Malaysian Insider*, 24 September 2013, accessed 28 June 2014.

5. Felix Oberholzer-Gee, 'A Market for Time Fairness and Efficiency in Waiting Lines,' Crema Center for Research in Economics, Management and the Arts at Harvard University, September 2003, 16, http://www.crema-research. ch/papers/2003-04.pdf, accessed 28 June 2014.

6. *Game Theory and Queue-jumpers*

1. Andrew X. Pham, *Catfish and Mandala: A Two-Wheeled Voyage through the Landscape and Memory of Vietnam* (New York: Picador, 1999).

2. Gad Allon and Eran Hanany, 'Cutting in Line: Social Norms in Queues,' MSOM Annual Conference, Ann Arbor, Michigan, 26-28 June 2011, 2.

3. Ibid, 1.

4. B. Schwartz, *Queuing and Waiting* (Chicago: University of Chicago Press, 1975).

7. *The Theory of Queue-jumping Mid-traffic*

1. Strangely, we almost never see a single traffic cop on the scene trying to fine the lane violators. There is neither self-regulation amongst the motorists nor regulation enforced by law. In these technology-enabled days, why shouldn't we have cameras which photograph wrongdoers, on the basis of which tickets can be sent to their homes?

2. Temptation, Reward, Penalty and Sucker's Pay-off are terms originally used by Martin Gardner.

3. 'Bag-drop queues as long as check-in,' Which? News, 17 August 2013.

8. *An Imaginative Case of Queue-jumping*

1. Radhika Vaz, 'Bum Whisperer: Solving the mystery of standing body to body at airports,' *Times of India*, 28 October 2014, http://blogs.timesofindia.indiatimes.com/read-it-and-weep/bum-whisperer-solving-the-mystery-of-standing-body-to-body-at-airports/, accessed 30 April 2016.
2. For a more detailed list of companies for which cheat sheets are provided, see http://harpweb.com/trivia/getpastvoicemail.html.
3. 'How to cheat call centre queues,' http://www.thisismoney.co.uk/money/bills/article-1605285/How-to-cheat-call-centre-queues.html, accessed 30 April 2016.
4. 'How to cheat call centre queues,' http://www.thisismoney.co.uk/money/bills/article-1605285/How-to-cheat-call-centre-queues.html, accessed 27 October 2014.

9. *Professional Queuers and Queue-jumping*

1. 'China's professional queuers paid to stand around,' National Public Radio (Online), 25 July 2011, http://www.npr.org/2011/07/25/138549322/chinas-professional-queuers-paid-to-stand-around, accessed 30 April 2016.
2. 'Italy's patient man: Graduate will queue for you – for €10 an hour,' *Guardian*, 29 January 2014, http://www.theguardian.com/world/2014/jan/29/italy-patient-man-graduate-queuer-milan-giovanni-cafaro, accessed 30 April 2016.
3. Michael J. Sandel, *What Money Can't Buy: The Moral Limits of Markets* (London: Penguin Books, 2012): 20.
4. Geert Hofstede & Michael H. Bond, 'Hofstede's Culture

Dimensions,' Journal of Cross-Cultural Psychology (December 1984): 417-33.

5. Geert Hofstede, 'Dimensionalizing Cultures: The Hofstede Model in Context,' 12 January 2011, http://scholarworks.gvsu. edu/cgi/viewcontent.cgi?article=1014&context=orpc, accessed 30 April 2016.

6. Michael J. Sandel, What Money Can't Buy: The Moral Limits of Markets (London: Penguin Books, 2012): 21.

7. Ibid, 22-23

8. Ibid.

10. *Ethics of Queue-jumping for the Scrupulous*

1. Marty Lariviere, 'The Ethics of Jumping the Queue,' *The Operations Room*, 27 August 2012, http://operationsroom. wordpress.com/2012/08/27/the-ethics-of-jumping-the-queue/, accessed 1 January 2015.

2. 'Calgary surgeon says broken system led to queue-jumping,' CBC News, 10 January 2013, http://www.cbc.ca/news/canada/ calgary/calgary-surgeon-says-broken-system-led-to-queue-jumping-1.1303168, accessed 23 April 2014.

Index

Acknowledgements

The seeds of this book are perhaps as old as Indians' propensity to jump queues. In this sense, this was a book waiting to happen all along. In the course of writing it, I have wondered if I was per chance writing a sequel to *Games Indians Play* after a decade of dwelling on the idea. But I am now convinced that this is not so. Queue-jumping, even if we hate to admit it, is a national trait, and it could not simply be allowed to pass without a book commenting on it in its own right. So that's what it is.

There are many in the queue whom I would like to thank heartily for making this book happen. Meena, my best buddy (also my wife), is almost always the first in line. She is always the first to work on my clumsy drafts, plodding through version after version, bringing the manuscript to a stage where I can dare send it to the publishers. And then there are two guinea pigs to whom I am indebted for encouraging comments on my early drafts. They are Ravi, my brother, and Sushma, an avid reader. I owe no less gratitude towards my countrymen at large, for, without their queue-jumping propensity, this book would never have been possible.

Acknowledgements

There is no way I can adequately thank my very good friend Nilofer Suleman, who voluntarily offered to do the cover art for the book with a little help from her hugely talented daughter Shilo Shiv Suleman. I remain indebted to them both.

I am also deeply grateful to Krishan Chopra, Publisher and Chief Editor at HarperCollins, whose invaluable comments on the first draft of the manuscript went a long way in improving the book, and to Siddhesh Inamdar, copy editor, but for whose painstaking editing the book would have been far less readable. Of course, any shortcomings are mine and only mine.

Finally, I owe a big thanks to our many institutions – whether businesses, airports, railway stations or government offices – all of which were ready laboratories to observe our collective queue-jumping behaviour.